Clutter Clearing Choices

Clear Clutter, Organize Your
Home, & Reclaim Your Life

First published by O Books, 2010
O Books is an imprint of John Hunt Publishing Ltd., The Bothy, Deershot Lodge, Park Lane, Ropley,
Hants, SO24 0BE, UK
office1@o-books.net
www.o-books.net

Distribution in:	South Africa
	Stephan Phillips (pty) Ltd
UK and Europe	Email: orders@stephanphillips.com
Orca Book Services	Tel: 27 21 4489839 Telefax: 27 21 4479879
orders@orcabookservices.co.uk	
Tel: 01202 665432 Fax: 01202 666219	
Int. code (44)	Text copyright Barbara Tako 2008
	Design: Stuart Davies
USA and Canada	
NBN	ISBN: 978 1 84694 262 4
custserv@nbnbooks.com	
Tel: 1 800 462 6420 Fax: 1 800 338 4550	All rights reserved. Except for brief quotations
	in critical articles or reviews, no part of this
	book may be reproduced in any manner without
Australia and New Zealand	prior written permission from the publishers.
Brumby Books	
sales@brumbybooks.com.au	
Tel: 61 3 9761 5535 Fax: 61 3 9761 7095	The rights of Barbara Tako as author have been
	asserted in accordance with the Copyright,
Far East (offices in Singapore, Thailand,	Designs and Patents Act 1988.
Hong Kong, Taiwan)	
Pansing Distribution Pte Ltd	
kemal@pansing.com	A CIP catalogue record for this book is available
Tel: 65 6319 9939 Fax: 65 6462 5761	from the British Library.

Printed by Digital Book Print

O Books operates a distinctive and ethical publishing philosophy in
all areas of its business, from its global network of authors to
production and worldwide distribution.

Clutter Clearing Choices

Clear Clutter, Organize Your Home, & Reclaim Your Life

Barbara Tako

BOOKS

Winchester, UK
Washington, USA

CONTENTS

Dedication   xi
Acknowledgements   xii
Disclaimer   xii
Foreword   1

Introductions and Basics   **3**
It all started...   3
What is clutter?   4
Gosh, where did all this stuff come from?   4
Why decide to work on clutter?   5
The history of clutter control help.   6
Why this book?   7

Section 1 Winter   **9**
Chapter 1   New Year's Resolution: First Resolve to
             Take Care of You   10
Chapter 2   More Simple New Year's Resolutions:
             Less is More   13
Chapter 3   As Simple As It Gets: One New Year's
             Resolution   16
Chapter 4   The Birth of the Underwear Drawer Lady   18
Chapter 5   Cure Household Chaos: As Simple As One,
             Two Three!   21
Chapter 6   Closet Clutter Be Gone!   24
Chapter 7   Simple Solutions for the Winter Blahs   27
Chapter 8   Unclutter Mantras & Methods   28
Chapter 9   Simplified Cooking   31
Chapter 10   Sadly Sorting Socks & Solving Laundry Woes   36
Chapter 11   Toy Clutter after the Christmas Holidays   40
Chapter 12   Living Room or Family Room: Organize Our
             Winter Habitat   43

Chapter 13   Clutter & Cleaning Products   46
Chapter 14   Air Clutter: A Breath of Fresh Air   48
Chapter 15   What About Inherited Clutter?   51
Chapter 16   Uncluttered Organization Means Functional
             Storage Containers   54
Chapter 17   Seek Help for Life Clutter   57
Chapter 18   Want to Make Changes? First, Get "Unstuck"   59
Chapter 19   Whatever You Do, Don't Quit: "Just Keep
             Swimming"   61
Chapter 20   People Clutter?   63
Chapter 21   Valentine's Day & Life Priorities   66
Chapter 22   Valentine's Day Gift: A Professional
             Organizer   69
Chapter 23   Did You Get What You Wanted for
             Valentine's Day?   72

Section 2 Spring   75
Chapter 1   Get Clutter Help from Spouse and Kids?   76
Chapter 2   Cleaning Tools, Procrastination, &
             Perfectionism   81
Chapter 3   Spring Cleaning—To Clean or Not to Clean   83
Chapter 4   Know This *BEFORE* You Spring Clean:
             Donation Values   87
Chapter 5   One Person's Trash is Another Person's
             Treasure: Responsible Donating   89
Chapter 6 · Candy, Candy, Candy: Children's Easter
             Clutter   91
Chapter 7   Body Clutter: The "D" Word—Diet!   94
Chapter 8   Clutter Clearing Home Decorating Ideas   97
Chapter 9   Potholes & Priorities—Keep an Eye on the Big
             Picture   102
Chapter 10   Clutter Again—Peeling Back the Layers   105
Chapter 11   Commen Sense Clutter Control   108

Chapter 12 Garage Sale Shopping—One Mom's Idea of
            Fashion, Fun, & Frugality   111
Chapter 13 Have a Garage Sale: Turn Clutter into Cash   117
Chapter 14 Consumerism Doesn't Clear Clutter   122
Chapter 15 Daily Paper Clutter   125
Chapter 16 "Moving Piles" of Paper Clutter   129
Chapter 17 Organize Long-Term Paper   131
Chapter 18 Purge Long-Term Paper Clutter   134
Chapter 19 Photo Clutter—Photos, Photos, & More
            Unsorted Photos   137

Section 3 Summer   **141**
Chapter 1   Lawn Furniture Clutter—Maybe   142
Chapter 2   Unclutter Summer Yard Work   144
Chapter 3   Children Unclutter My Life—No Kidding!   147
Chapter 4   The Toy Lesson   150
Chapter 5   The Hub of the Home: Reduce Kitchen
            Clutter   153
Chapter 6   Don't "Kill" Celery Again—Clear Refrigerator
            Clutter   156
Chapter 7   Kitchen Organizing—Get Out of the Kitchen
            and Outside!   159
Chapter 8   What is a Clutter Buddy?   163
Chapter 9   Household CHAOS: Real or Perceived?   165
Chapter 10 A Simple Family Vacation—Not So Simple   168
Chapter 11 Happy 4th of July: Unclutter Your Personal
            Historical Treasures   172
Chapter 12 The Paper Air Plane: Children's Trash or
            Treasure?   175
Chapter 13 Slow Down Summer!   178
Chapter 14 The Swimming Lesson: Quality Time or
            Quantity Time?   182
Chapter 15 Clear Hectic Fall Schedule Clutter Now   185
Chapter 16 Organize Your Fall Time: Goal Setting   188

Section 4 Fall   **193**

Chapter 1   Practical Time Management   194

Chapter 2   Time Management Tips for Fall   197

Chapter 3   When Time Management Techniques Fail:
Tough Choices to Unclutter Life   201

Chapter 4   June Cleaver's Fall Cleaning Routines:
What is Her Secret?   204

Chapter 5   School Paper Organization for the Parentally
Piled Upon   207

Chapter 6   Love Yourself & Your Family: Weed Out
Before Winter   211

Chapter 7   Sneaky Stuff: Zap "Hidden" Clutter this Fall   214

Chapter 8   Mental Tools to Clear Clutter   217

Chapter 9   The Bathroom Battle—Soap Scum &
Mirror Smears   220

Chapter 10   Inner Simplicity: Have an Internal Garage
Sale this Fall   224

Chapter 11   Use It Or Lose It   226

Chapter 12   Children's Clutter: Trick or Treat Under My
Children's Beds?   228

Chapter 13   Halloween Clutter: This Is Halloween, Not
Christmas!   231

Chapter 14   Frugal Financial Choices   233

Chapter 15   Clear your Home Entryway of Fall & Winter
Clutter   237

Chapter 16   A Thanksgiving Opinion: Don't Overstuff
Your Turkey or Your Home   240

Chapter 17   Thanksgiving: Simplifying Holidays Just
Isn't Simple   243

Chapter 18   A Not-So-Perfect Holiday Table: Sometimes
Stuff Isn't Clutter   246

Chapter 19   Let's Talk Turkey: Clear the Clutter, Keep
the Gratitude   248

Section 5 Christmas Season **251**

Chapter 1   Panic Attack: Fewer than 25 Shopping
            Days Left? Fight Back: Clear Clutter & Focus   252
Chapter 2   Shop 'Til You Drop or Simplify Christmas
            Shopping?   256
Chapter 3   Give the Gift of Time   260
Chapter 4   Clutter Cures for the Seasonal "Gimmes"   262
Chapter 5   Does the Christmas Cookie Crumble or
            Do I Fold?   265
Chapter 6   Follow Your Gut: Try a Guilt-Free Holiday
            this Year   268
Chapter 7   The Short & Simple Route to an Uncluttered
            Christmas   271

**Conclusion: Clutter Free – Freed up to Live
            Life's Experiences** **273**

Chapter 1   Necessary Isn't Always Clutter-Free   274
Chapter 2   The Heart of Clutter-Free Living—What
            Really Matters?   277
Chapter 3   The Minimalist Finds Peace   280

Author Contact Information **282**

Bibliography & Further Reading and Website Resources **283**

Dedicated to

Daniel, Emily, & Sarah

Acknowledgements

I am thankful for the support of everyone around me who helped make this book happen.

I am grateful to John Hunt and the rest of the terrific staff at O Books.

Many thanks also to the members of the simple living group and the attendees of my seminars and classes over the years for your questions, ideas, and valuable insights.

I am especially grateful for the support and encouragement of my friends Laura Hutton, Jennifer & Jason Lassner, Arvilla & Dan Cadwell, Denise Yanara, T. Aaron Ridge, Pam Marta, Paulette Henderson, Tricia McCloy, Cheryl Kargel, Jackie Dimmick, Barb Nevin, Rachel Hanson, Mary & Sherman Anderson, Lee Ann Schutz, Jan Catton, Carla Hibbison, Barbara Thompson, Diane Bailey, and Linda Woyke.

You guys are the best.

Without the encouragement and love of family including David & Anne Seltzer, George & Lucille Tako, Jim Tako, Jan Tako, and Nicole Tako, this book would never have happened. Thank you.

Most of all, to my husband Dan and my daughters Emily and Sarah, please accept my thanks beyond words. It was your love and support that ultimately made this happen.

FOREWORD

After six years of marriage, my wife Sandy and I are finally living under one roof and blending all our accumulated stuff from maintaining two households in two different communities. Being knee deep in clutter, Barbara Tako's book *Clutter Clearing Choices: Clear Clutter, Organize Your Home, and Reclaim Your Life*, is a God send!

Tako organizes her book by season starting with winter and New Year's resolutions to take better care of oneself and to get organized. Then it is spring cleaning and body clutter, including the "D" word; dieting. Next is dealing with summer lawn furniture, uncluttering yard work, and an admonition: Don't kill celery; clear the refrigerator clutter. For the fall season there are chapters entitled *Love Yourself and Your Family: Weed out before Winter,* and *Inner Simplicity: Have an Internal Garage Sale this Fall.* Tako has wonderful advice on how to simplify without guilt for the Christmas season and concludes the book with a chapter on what really matters. Here she describes being with her grand-father at the end of his life, and shares these thoughts about simple, clutter free living: "Clutter clearing choices can help simplify life. What does this simplified life look like? The heart of simple living is about love. I learned to let control, cleaning, organizing, and overscheduled daily life and almost everything else go. Clutter-free living is taking care of people you love and living what you believe." The final chapter entitled *The Minimalist Finds Peace* sums up the details of the book—clutter is anything in my life that weighs me down. Clearing the "clutter" is about freeing me for intentional, simple living.

Tako has a warm and personal style of writing which helps the reader to identify with her and with her struggles and successes at organizing and clearing clutter. This is not an overbearing one way for all people self help book, but a series of conversations with a friend about things that matter—about clearing away what weighs you down, taking care of the people you love and living what you believe. This is a book I will come back to many times as the seasons change, as the cleaning bug strikes, and as a reminder about what is truly important in life.

The Reverend Michael Mortvedt,
Co-Director of Alternatives for Simple Living

ALTERNATIVES for Simple Living
0038 Deer Path Rd.
PO Box 3804
Dillon, CO 80435-3804

800.821.6153
970/468-AFSL (2375)
970/333-9032 - cell
970/513-6883 - fax

Alternatives@SimpleLiving.org
www.SimpleLiving.org

INTRODUCTIONS AND THE BASICS

It all started…

It all started the moment it dawned on me that truth is sometimes more entertaining than fiction and that helpful ideas might be more easily digested if they come from someone who is a 'real' person rather than a perfect person.

Hey, this could be a good fit – 365 days per year, I am way too real — just ask my kids.

What if some unsuspecting woman from a much earlier time found her consciousness suddenly swapped with mine? She would find herself stuck in the body of a less-than-perfect housewife, mother, and sometimes works-outside-the-home woman trapped in suburbia. Would she be happy with her newfound overabundance of modern prosperity? Would she find it enlightening to try to operate the electric toothbrush, the programmable microwave, the dishwasher, the washer / dryer, the car, the busy spouse, and over-scheduled children? Or would she find herself rapidly frustrated, overwhelmed, confused, and longing for a less cluttered and simpler life?

I claim to crave a simpler life, but I am faulty and confused. I like gadgets, hot showers, modern conveniences, and living in a land of opportunity. I don't like to cook, and I hate to fold laundry. I am tired of getting the kitchen floor wet every time I empty the dishwasher, and I find it easier to ignore paperwork than to deal with it—especially if it involves retirement planning or ideas about saving for my children's education.

I enjoy learning how to get better at making life choices, and I work hard on clutter clearing choices and household organizing. I have been teaching, writing, and helping thousands of others with this for over a decade. Hence, this book.

Why do I spend so much time working on clutter control? It may be because I tend to be a "glass is half empty" sort of a person. I will spend most of my life waiting for the other shoe to drop. I conclude that if I am *not* waist-deep in clutter, I will be better prepared to cope when Life's shoes drop on me.

I also am lazy. I want to spend time on my priorities rather than time hunting for permission slips, car keys, matching shoes, or a return receipt.

There are other people out there who want to get rid of clutter and make clutter clearing choices in many life areas. We can learn together. A simpler more clutter-free life is out there waiting for us; but first, let's cover the basics:

What is clutter?

- Clutter is anything in my life that isn't helpful to me.
- Clutter is physical, mental, emotional, and relational.
- Clutter can be tangible like household goods, clothing, toys, and paperwork.
- Clutter can also be feelings that pull us down and wear us out, including stress, guilt, anxiety, depression, and postponed decisions about paperwork and other stuff in our lives.
- Clutter can even include poisonous relationships with other people.
- Clutter is stuff in my life that needs to be resolved or to go away.

It is no longer beautiful, useful, or has sentimental value. Clutter is stuff that no longer enriches my life. The cost for keeping this stuff no longer outweighs the benefit of letting it go.

Gosh, where did all this stuff come from?

How did I get into clutter trouble? Where did all the clutter come from? It came from stores, Internet shopping, garage sales, gifts, hand-me-downs, and well-meaning family members, friends, and neighbors.

I have too much stuff. Other people may feel this way too. There are too many choices, opportunities, and things out there. Unfortunately, the thing we often have too little of is time. Life is overwhelming. I am under-whelmed and over-whelmed by my clutter. I don't need all this stuff to be happy. In fact, the sheer quantity makes me unhappy. It's a physical, emotional, financial, and spiritual drain to keep, clean, store, and maintain all of this stuff. It isn't peaceful, and I crave peace.

When did I get into clutter trouble? I didn't suddenly get all this stuff, so I won't be able to make it go away suddenly either. Clutter control is a process and a series of new habits that I have had to learn. There is not a quick do-it-once-and-it's-done solution to clutter. (If you have one, then *you* please write a book.)

Clutter comes from our behavior. We shop. We keep gifts out of respect or affection for the giver. We cling to old organizing habits in spite of life changes that would be better served by new organizing techniques. We hang onto stuff because we "paid good money for it," or it still has some "life in it," or it "could" still be "useful" or just because we "should." We put weeding out and organizing low on our priority list. And after a while, we find ourselves buried in our clutter.

Why decide to work on clutter?

I accidentally made the right choice (the decision to work on my clutter) for the wrong reason. I was trying to keep up with my mother-in-law, who, frankly, intimidated me. My mother-in-law could make June Cleaver from the old television series *Leave It To Beaver* look like a slob.

There was rarely a piece of mail on her kitchen counter or a dust bunny lurking in the corner of her bathroom or anywhere else in her home. It didn't matter what day of the week or time of day we stopped by. Her home was neat, orderly, and clutter-free. What was her secret? I didn't know, but I wanted to keep up with her.

When she would come to visit our home, I would toss things into closets and drawers to hide our clutter. I felt my home should look as nice as my mother-in-law's did. As long as I had enough time to prepare, and she didn't look in the coat closet or open a drawer, I could keep up appearances. Unfortunately, that was all I was doing. I wanted to do something more.

My fear of her housekeeping practices gradually turned to admiration. Because she was better organized and had less junk than many of us, she had the time and energy for her priorities — her church, family, friends, and hobbies. My mother-in-law is an awesome person who taught me that clutter control and home organizing aren't ends in themselves. They are the means to free up time and energy for our personal priorities — whether they are spiritual, relationship, career-oriented, or anything else. Getting rid of clutter is a means to an end, and I want it!

If you aren't ready to address clutter yet, that is okay too. When you are ready to get rid of the clutter, you will do it. It is that simple. Don't beat yourself up if you aren't ready. Get on with your life, and check back with yourself periodically to see if the time is right to get rid of clutter. There is lots of available clutter control help when you are ready.

The history of clutter control help

The first books on clutter provided techniques to get rid of clutter. Naturally organized people wrote some of these books. These folks sometimes frustrated the rest of us less organized folks who could not keep up with all of their clever systems for staying organized. Technique alone did not appear to be the answer.

Later, clutter technique books got better at explaining basic organizing techniques, however they continued to assume that clutter was the disease and that cutting it out would cure it. Why, after weeding out, does the clutter keep coming back? Clearly, there is more to staying clutter-free than simply learning how to toss clutter into the bin.

Subsequent books observed that different personality styles dealt with clutter differently and suggested using different styles or techniques for getting rid of clutter for different people. These books also offered different styles for comfortably organizing what was left. It was important that personality or personal style was now a recognized factor in the clutter-clearing arena.

Still other books taught us that our attachment to various clutter could be a product of underlying psychological and emotional issues. If we could resolve our underlying "issues" we could get rid of our clutter. Hence, another important piece of the puzzle fell into place.

More recent books start to acknowledge that life changes could cause a person's organizing systems to break down and cause clutter. These books point out that organizing systems need to change over time to accommodate changing life circum-stances. The recognition that clutter control is an ongoing process that needs to adapt to life changes is critical.

So, which books are right? All of them! There are excellent technique books available to get rid of clutter. There are specific techniques to stay organized to fit your personal organizing style. There are underlying psychological issues that impact our attachments to stuff and recognizing those will help us part with our stuff. And, finally, there are constant life changes that regularly derail our current organizing systems. Clutter clearing really is a lifelong process.

Why this book?

My goal is to help people get rid of clutter — physical, mental, emotional, time robbing clutter.

I believe clutter clearing is one piece of a simpler and more peaceful life. I want to help people make their own clutter clearing choices in a variety of life areas to free up time and energy for their own priorities. Some people crave inner peace and realize that outer order can help them achieve it. Sometimes we have too many loose ends constantly spinning around in our heads.

Life is often complicated. If our homes are clutter free and organized, it can help quiet our inner turmoil so we can focus on our priorities, whatever they are for each of us.

I hope this book will help us learn to whittle away at clutter together. I don't have all the answers. I do share small pieces of the puzzle in manageable bits, and if you look at the Further Reading section at the end of the book, you will see some very helpful books and websites to pursue these topics in greater detail.

I have chosen a short chapter format within each season of the year. I have organized it seasonally because many of us tend to think about different kinds of clutter in our lives during specific seasons of the year. I have used the words "house" and "home" interchangeably, and I intend them to apply to apartments, condominiums, townhouses, houses... anywhere *your home* is. I also have used she or he in this book with no intentions of gender specificity in regards to clutter management. You are welcome to start at the beginning or to start with the season that you are in.

Please take your time. Clutter clearing is a process. Ponder and work at your own pace. Let your own uniqueness help you choose your path. Feel free to skip and ignore stuff that doesn't fit where you are right now. Pick and choose what works for you. Leave the procrastination, perfectionism, and especially the guilt behind.

There is no "one right way" to clear clutter from our lives, so consider this to be a buffet where you can pick, choose what you want, and spring board with your own ideas. You can do this. You can clear the clutter from your life and free up time for your priorities.

Ready, set, go!

~

Section 1

Winter

~

CHAPTER 1

NEW YEAR'S RESOLUTION: FIRST RESOLVE TO TAKE CARE OF YOU

Have I seen you? Are you the tired person in line at the gas station, the person with glazed eyes, trying to find a parking space at the crowded grocery store, or the tense person charging quickly through the mall?

Pulling off the holidays isn't simple. It is easy to get worn down. How can you recharge yourself if your battery is burned out? Are you too busy taking care of others to take care of yourself?

Self-care doesn't come easily in these hectic times, especially if you suffer from self-care guilt. Many of us are comfortable taking care of other people, but we feel guilty at the thought of spending any time, energy, or money on ourselves. Self-care often comes last, if at all, on the long "to do" list. After I get done at work, after I get groceries, after I take the kids to practice, after I get the oil changed, after I clean up the kitchen... After, after, after until "after" becomes "never." And we get sick.

Since it is that time of year again — the annual making and breaking of New Year's Resolutions, I decided to suggest a few simple self-care resolutions. After all, you really can't do your best at taking care of anyone or anything in your life until you also take care of yourself. Now if that really is such a common sense statement, how come you're still so tired and stressed out?

First, resolve to take care of the basics — this year and every year. It is a new calendar year. Schedule annual physicals, dental exams, and eye exams for you and other family members now. While you are at it, consider scheduling time for enough sleep, a little exercise, and maybe include plans to make a few food changes that start you on a healthier path.

Second, make a resolution to put something just for you on your weekly "to do" lists this year, and make sure you do them. Maybe there are places you want to go, restaurants you want to try, or projects you'd like to do for fun. Give yourself permission to put that special thing just for you on your weekly "to do" list with all of the other stuff that *has* to get done.

Third, make some breathing space for yourself to figure out what you want to do this year to take care of yourself physically, emotionally, or spiritually. If you don't pause to figure it out, no one else will figure it out for you. Do you need to lose weight or exercise? Do you need to stay better connected with friends or family? Do you need to get in tune with your spirituality? Only you know what you need most.

There are also some books if you are looking for ideas on self-care. For moms and dads, I suggest a book that can give you the gift of time. It is called *Mommy Time — 101 great ways to keep your child entertained while you get something else done* by Danelle Hickman & Valerie Teurlay.

For women or men (in spite of the gender wording in the title), I also suggest *The Woman's Comfort Book* by Jennifer Louden or *The Woman's Retreat Book*, which is also written by Jennifer Louden. Whether you have five minutes, five hours, or five days, both of these books have ideas for nurturing yourself that you may find more restoring than vegging out in front of the television.

If the Internet is your thing, you can find help there too. Sign up for a free monthly resolution reminder email that includes links specifically geared toward the resolutions you selected. You can do this at: www.hiaspire.com/newyear. If your budget is tight after the holidays www.allthingsfrugal.com/resolutions. htm might help, it offers action plan goal ideas for various life areas.

Finally, remember to be kind to yourself. We are all creatures of habit. Dropping bad habits or cultivating new ones takes time and effort. Don't take on too much all at once. Pick two or three things for the year. Remember if you don't succeed this year, you'll get another chance next year.

CHAPTER 2

MORE SIMPLE NEW YEAR'S RESOLUTIONS: LESS IS MORE

What? Is it the second day of January and you already broke your New Year's resolution? After all those holiday goodies, did your resolution to lose weight find you standing at the refrigerator door, tired, hungry and ready to graze, by 2pm on New Year's Day?

Or, did you decide to take on the whole world this year? Did you make a pile of resolutions in your head that were designed to make your life better, faster, and stronger? Have you already dropped or forgotten so many of these resolutions that you wonder why you even bothered to make them?

Is there a better way to make those darn New Year's resolutions work? I don't know. I hope so. I do know there is a simpler way, of course. My ideas track with KISS — "keep it simple, silly." Here are three thoughts to help make resolutions really happen.

First, I vowed this year to skip the attempt to fix my whole life. I will stare the American Dream to "have it all" in the face and say "not so fast." I don't want to shoot for working on everything and wind up accomplishing nothing. Another year goes by and I find myself in the same place I was before. Instead of a dozen good intentions, I will focus on one or two resolutions that are really important to me this year and I will achieve them.

Think about broad life goal areas (career, relationship, spiritual, community service, financial, social, personal, and health). What life area bugs you the most or is your highest priority? Create one or two resolutions based on these.

Stop at only one or two resolutions so you can remember

13

them, focus on them, and actually get them accomplished. I don't want to keep repeating the same well-intentioned resolutions year after year. I want to get them done and get on with the rest of my life.

Let's say that I'd like to address my health, and my personal development goal areas. It really bugs me that I can't button some of my pants right now, and it frustrates me that I claim, in my head, to value personal development but I rarely make the time to do it.

Next, design whatever resolutions you pick as goals: Make them specific, measurable, and doable. If I resolve to lose weight or spend more time on personal development, I have to be clear about how it will happen. Better resolutions for me might be: I will lose fifteen pounds by May 1st. And, I will take two personal retreats this year. It will be much easier to track, measure, and achieve success if it is clear what I have to do to accomplish my resolutions.

Finally, make resolutions that really excite you! If you aren't thrilled or motivated to accomplish these resolutions, what's the point?

Pick resolutions that fire you up. For example, I would love to take a break from my regular routine and take a weekend retreat. Major changes and new life directions have come from previous personal retreats for me.

If you merely pick resolutions from your "should do" list or items that society's expectations have foisted onto you, how far will you really try to get? Maybe there is something more important to me right now than weight loss (society's expectation that I be thinner).

Work on resolutions that are your passion. I suspect you might agree that following your passion is part of a happier and more peaceful life. Don't you feel more fulfilled when you spend time working on what you really love? Time really does fly when you are having fun.

If a resolution isn't intrinsically motivating, consider creating an exciting reward for yourself for achieving it. (I suppose I would do better if I could find the thought of my pants fitting to be exciting, but I usually can't make that vision as exciting to me as a plate of delicious food!) Make the reward something that is a real treat for you. Withhold the treat until you achieve your resolution. If I achieve my weight goal, I could promise myself lunch at a special restaurant.

Yes, I'm aware of the irony of having dining out as the reward for a weight loss goal, but what can I say? I am passionate about food! The point is to make the reward truly special for you, not something you already periodically enjoy. Make sure that the resolution or the reward or both are a passion for you.

If my New Year's resolutions are simple — limited to one or two, clearly defined, and exciting to me, I have a better shot at making them finally happen. When I get them done, I can pick something new for next year!

CHAPTER 3

AS SIMPLE AS IT GETS: ONE NEW YEAR'S RESOLUTION

Is there one simple New Year's resolution that could improve everyone's life? Maybe I've lost it – who'd dare to think there is a one-size-fits-all answer to life that would make everyone happy? Hah! But, pondering this brought up a related question that deserves some thought: Why do some people find peace, happiness and success while other people fail? Why, when bad things happen, do some folks suffer while other folks make lemonade? I want to find the answer and make it my New Year's resolution.

Why do some of us hang up in frustration when we've been put on hold for the fourth time and other people persist? Why can some veterans come home from war and function fine while others struggle? Why do some people with a debilitating disease exude grace and peace while others are overwhelmed?

I recently asked a special needs teacher about kids who come from troubled families. I asked her why some kids from a tough background or family situation make it while others don't. Her response was: **resilience**. She felt some kids simply had more natural resilience than others had and could therefore overcome life's negative events better.

Resilience is defined in my Merriam-Webster's dictionary as "the capability of a strained body to recover its size and shape after deformation caused by compressive stress" or "an ability to recover from or adjust easily to misfortune or change." This sounds like a quality we'd all like to have. These definitions remind me of a foam rubber ball. I want to be more like a foam rubber ball.

My New Year's resolution for this year is simple. I am going to try to be more resilient. Is that possible if resilience is an ability or an innate quality? Yes, I think so.

First, I am going to work to make countless choices to be resilient when life kicks up the usual problems throughout the year.

I am a huge believer in the power of choice. I believe that we, as people, have the power to choose. I think we all can make better or different choices on a daily basis. For example, when my kids are stomping around the house and arguing, I can choose to yell at them or I can try to approach the situation calmly.

Second, I am going to surround myself with things that help me be resilient. I appreciate nature. It is big. I am small. I sometimes simply take an outdoor walk to help me regain perspective. Owning a dog also helps me to be resilient. Coming home to unconditional puppy love every day definitely improves my resiliency. Figure out what people/pets/activities/things help you to be more resilient and surround yourself with them. Focus on them.

Third, I am going to work on my attitude. If I can't change events, I can still change how I perceive them and how I choose to react to them. Is the glass half empty or half full? When the garage door spring breaks in the middle of winter, am I going to panic or problem solve? Am I going to be grateful for what's going right in my life or am I going to dwell on the stuff that upsets me?

What would happen if we all worked to be more resilient? I think it would be amazing. Instead of banging into each other and coming away shattered, cracked, bent, or broken, we would bounce away like a foam rubber ball and come back whole and ready for the next adventure! Wouldn't that be a positive New Year's resolution?

CHAPTER 4

THE BIRTH OF THE UNDERWEAR DRAWER LADY

Where can you turn to stay motivated on your clutter control journey?

Simple pleasures are the most enduring ones. My underwear drawer makes me happy. There can be mounds of toys on the living room floor, piles of papers on the kitchen table, and dirty dishes in the sink, but I can be content. A small part of my world still has order. My simple tidy underwear drawer survives even the worst days.

Here is how I did it. One day I got realistic. I completely emptied out my underwear drawer. It was the only way to really see what I had since it was crammed full. It had been no fun to try to put neatly folded laundry into this jammed up drawer.

First, I let go of the **past**: I tossed out my frilly slinky shower gift items that had only been worn a few times early in our marriage.

Next, I let go of a **life stage**: I pitched maternity underwear.

Gratefully, I released the **guilt** (yes, there was guilt-ridden underwear): I got rid of the pre-children underwear — yes, it is okay that I probably won't be that size again. I don't have to feel bad every morning when I dig through my drawer looking for something that currently fits! Finally, I threw out the **worn-out stuff**: You know, the underwear I wouldn't want to be seen in, at a hospital emergency room (or in my case, I didn't want to entertain the camera person at the mall store, if I decided to clothes shop later). You know the last kind of underwear, the ones you can poke your fingers through at the hips every time you pull them up.

What was I left with? Paradise! Several sets of decent underwear that were in reasonable shape. They fit me and they now fit in the drawer! I grabbed a couple of cardboard shoeboxes. Tops in one. Bottoms in the other. Now I even had room in the drawer to spare.

The phone can ring off the hook. The kids can cry in tandem. The pot on the stove can bubble over. But now, one tiny spot in my life stays calm. It is self-maintaining too. The boxes keep things from getting stirred together again in the drawer. An unstuffed drawer now makes it fun and easy to put clean laundry away. And, if one of the boxes starts to get too full, I can instantly see it is time to weed out the most worn-out stuff in the box.

Imagine what would happen if everyone had a calm spot, an oasis like this, in their lives. Better yet, what if they expanded this simple peace to their sock drawer, their other drawers, and maybe even their closets?

Here are some basic thoughts for uncluttering and organizing:

Start small: Do one drawer or shelf at a time. A sock drawer could be straightened while you are on the phone. Spend only ten minutes a day, perhaps at the end of each day. Your dresser could be completed in a week.

Thin down: Less really can be more. Have more peace, energy, and time for the things that are important to you. You can donate your discards and have the satisfaction of knowing you are helping someone less fortunate than you are.

Be realistic about your life. If you do laundry once a week or more, why would you need 30 pairs of ... (you fill in the blank)?

Give yourself permission: Trim the excess and discover the pleasure of having only things that really bring you joy instead of guilt or sadness. Get rid of what doesn't fit, the stuff that you don't like, and the items you haven't found time to repair (and probably never will). Are you getting the idea?

Measure and plan: If you are going to buy or make smaller storage compartments, measure the stuff you want to store and the space you want to store it in. Don't stand in the store scratching your head and wondering if the cute plastic containers you've found will hold what you want, or fit in the drawer you plan to put them in!

Organize and maintain: Create a system that will keep things simple for you. The basic rule of organization is to divide to conquer. Smaller spaces, accomplished with drawer dividers, clear storage boxes, or extra shelving can work wonders in the limited spaces of our dressers and closets. Smaller compartments help keep quantities down by being a visual wake-up call when a compartment overflows. Compartmentalizing makes it easier to maintain order.

Find wasted or "lost" space: Drawer dividers will let you use the full height of the drawers because they keep items from tipping over onto each other. Extra shelving in closets can use the dead space above your current closet shelves and the forgotten middle space between the bottoms of your shirts on hangers and the floor.

My friends and students still laugh when I invite them to take a peek in my underwear (raised eyebrows) drawer. But many of them have gone home and a few weeks or months later found happiness in their own dresser drawers! This is the fun challenge. Will you give it a try? The gauntlet, or in this case, the sock, has been thrown.

CHAPTER 5

CURE HOUSEHOLD CHAOS: AS SIMPLE AS ONE, TWO, THREE!

When I married I discovered I had a wonderful mother-in-law. When she came to my house, I had to take her coat and throw it, with the others, on the bed. Even though my house was temporarily picked up for entertaining, I certainly wasn't going to let her or any of my other guests look in my closets!

After getting over my irrational fear of my tidy and well-organized mother-in-law, I decided she was onto something. Her closets, drawers, and everything else were clutter free and well organized. She had time for her priorities – her family, her friends, and her golfing.

My fear turned to admiration. How could I cure closet chaos too?

The Secret of Professional Organizers:
Primary, secondary and tertiary space and stuff. You can think like a professional organizer in your own home. I teach this organizing principle to my students. This organizing rule of thumb is: Primary stuff goes in primary space. Secondary stuff is kept in secondary space. And tertiary stuff can be put away somewhere that's harder to reach.

Primary space is space that is easy to get to. Primary stuff is stuff you use frequently. In a kitchen, primary space is from waist to shoulder height. That is why the cutlery drawer, which is used several times per day, is in primary space. Primary space is prime real estate — choice locations you use all the time because they are easy to reach and you spend your time there. The kitchen counter is prime real estate — only utensils used daily may live on the counter. Secondary stuff like dusty crock-pots, stand mixers, and used bread machines move into cupboards elsewhere.

Secondary space is less accessible. Reach up into a kitchen cupboard for a platter or bend down and take a pot from a lower cabinet to access secondary stuff stored in secondary space. If you use that crock-pot or bread machine weekly, they may live in secondary space.

Tertiary kitchen storage includes the cabinet above the refrigerator or the dead corner of a base cabinet. I used to go crawling in on my hands and knees into our base cabinet dead corner with a flashlight to look for my crock-pot and other "fun" surprises hidden there.

The problem was tertiary and secondary stuff creeping into my primary space. The bread maker I hadn't used in months lived on my kitchen counter! I wasn't using it, but I regularly had to move it to clean under it and wipe it down. I even had the audacity to complain about not having enough counter space.

I wasn't the only one complaining. My husband complained that his shirts were overcrowded on his side of our small bedroom closet. I discovered they were crushed together and bent at an angle on their hangers because his high school trombone was sitting at one end of his side of the closet. The trombone crowded his shirts and prevented them from hanging straight. I moved his trombone, which I know he will never part with, to a basement storage closet. He didn't notice the trombone was gone, but he quit complaining that his shirts were jammed in and wrinkled up in the closet.

I tell my students that I hope they won't find my husband's trombone in their closet. But, seriously, I do ask them to go home and look for their own "trombones." Maybe it will be the bocce ball set that crowded the boots all winter in the entryway closet. Maybe it will be the doughnut fryer in the kitchen cabinet that limits space for everyday pots and pans. Find your trombones. If you aren't willing to toss them, at least you can move them out of your primary space.

CHAPTER 6

CLOSET CLUTTER BE GONE!

To cure closet chaos, learn two techniques the pros use. All closet systems and organizers use these ideas. They use every square inch of storage space in closets – taking advantage of spaces overlooked by the rest of us. Second, they make stored items easy to reach and accessible to everyone who needs them (a critical concern unless you like maintaining all the closets in your home all by yourself).

To maximize closet space, put extra shelving in closets to use dead space above existing closet shelves. Add an extra shelf in every closet for excellent tertiary storage space throughout the home. Use the forgotten middle space between the bottom of shirts on hangers and the floor in bedroom closets. Do this by stacking storage boxes from the floor up through this "middle" storage space that is often just empty air space. Use hooks inside closets and hang things on the insides of closet doors. Any way to turn empty air space into functional storage is acceptable. Finally, go all the way to the floor with divided compartment storage containers, like divided shoeboxes or other stackable storage containers.

I recently watched some closet pros demonstrate their systems. They demonstrated how to create double hanging and how to maximize shelf and drawer storage space inside a closet. One system was adjustable. Adjustable shelves are important because storage needs change over time. Children's clothes get wider and longer as they grow. Adults change their minds as new hobbies, businesses, or clothing habits come into their lives.

There are professional closet systems, do-it-yourself kits from home supply stores, and stackable laminated wood boxes from retail stores that carry household products. And, of course, you can make your own by stacking up large plastic milk crates or large heavy-duty cardboard boxes.

It is important to make storage areas functional for everyone in my family. A good example was my small entryway closet. Remember a television series called *The Odd Couple*? As an organizer, I was an untidy Oscar pretending to be a very tidy Felix. I was motivated enough to try to jam a heavy Minnesota winter coat onto a flimsy metal dry cleaner style hanger and wedge it into the over-crowded tiny closet. I pushed the other coats to each side, quickly hung up my coat, and let the other coats slip back into place before my coat slid onto the floor. I called this elaborate technique the "pressure fit."

I am motivated enough to go through that process. Will the other people in my family put themselves through this? My spouse isn't going bother with it – and I don't blame him. He'll throw his coat on a chair or couch, explaining that he'll be going out again in a few hours (or days). As for my children? Well, they can't even reach the coat rod, much less perform the "pressure fit" maneuver.

Solutions: New rules, good equipment, and better habits

New rule: I limited each member of the family to two in-season coats in this closet at a time (Okay, I cheated, there are a couple of raincoats in there too). I also got rid of a lot of other things in the closet that didn't belong there.

Good equipment: I bought decent heavy-duty hangers that could handle the weight of heavy coats.

Finally, I installed some hooks (on a board that was supported by the solid edges of the hollow core door) that were at kid-height.

Now I had a small coat closet that was accessible and functional for everyone in my family. I even had a few decent hangers and a small amount of space for company coats!

Better habits: It took a couple of weeks to train my young children to use the new improved system. My spouse was thrilled enough by the heavy-duty hangers and extra closet space to help out.

Why do I believe in curing closet chaos? Am I digging through the box in the back of a closet to find my authentic self, to move on from the past, or simply to make functional storage space for all family members? Whatever the motivation, curing household chaos frees up time and space in my life for what is important to me, and now I can usually open my closets when company comes!

CHAPTER 7

SIMPLE SOLUTIONS FOR THE WINTER BLAHS

Sometimes the winter blahs hit with a vengeance. What is a poor, tired, cold person to do? Slow down! Come home from work and put on your pajama pants and sweatshirt. Burrow in. You aren't going anywhere tonight... Why not get comfortable?

Draw a hot bath and soak for a while. Pretend you are on a beach baking under the hot sun.

Turn off the television and take a nap. Curl up under a warm blanket with a soft pillow.

Go shopping at the library instead of the mall. Find a good book and go retreat with it.

Dig out a board game or puzzle. Find something to do other than the noise of the television or the flash of the computer screen.

Make homemade cookies so your home smells yummy!

Make hot cocoa. My kids often ask for this, yet, they rarely finish a cup. I don't know if they like the smell or the concept, or maybe just the melting marshmallows!

If you take this time to reflect, choose gratitude rather than frustration.

Do you want to curl up with a good book? Try *The Comfort Queen's Guide to Life—Create All That You Need With Just What You've Got* by Jennifer Louden.

Go to bed early. Almost everyone I've talked to lately seems extra tired. Why not hibernate? It is the season, after all.

CHAPTER 8

UNCLUTTER MANTRAS & METHODS

1. Saving my stuff won't save the memories. I can journal or use a photo album instead.
2. The quality of my family's life isn't improved by the quantity of stuff crammed in our closets. Less is more.
3. The less stuff I have, the easier it is for me to concentrate on the important stuff. I don't have to spend time handling, storing, cleaning, or even thinking about so much stuff.

When Walls Close in, Go Back to Basic Clutter Control

My home shrank after the holidays. Holiday clutter was basically put away, but my home felt cramped. When I watched my home slowly absorb all the gifts, the image that came to mind was a snake slowly swallowing a large rodent. As I looked further down the snake's body I saw other bulges where this had happened before.

I spend a lot of time working on clutter clearing, but when I go through my stuff, I still have trouble letting go. I have a weakness for saving. I have a problem with storing. I'm going to run out of storage space if I don't figure it out.

Sometimes I am afraid to toss stuff. When I finally weed out a few things, the familiar refrain "But I might need it someday..." plays over and over in my head. My weak spots include books, clothing, children's toys and art, stuff someone else gave me, kitchen gadgets, and knick-knacks.

Maybe my children will want this stuff someday. Maybe I'll finally organize those photos. Maybe I'll finally re-read those books Maybe I'll be that size again and then that outfit will magically fit and be in style too. ...Hah!

Here are three basic clutter control methods I turn to in my post-holiday frustration. Decide if any of them fits your time frame and personal style. There is no one right way to do it.

The 1-2-3-4(?) Box Method:

A standard method to weed out clutter is the three box method. It takes a full day or even a weekend to complete. Get three large boxes and work your way systematically from room to room. Place trash in the first box. Put items in decent enough condition to donate to a charity shop into the second box. Use the third box for things you find in one room that belong elsewhere. Items remain in the third box until you reach the room where they belong.

Maybe you wonder why you need the third box. Why not just put things back right away? This is why: when I find socks stuffed in the cracks of our family room sofa, I put them in the third box. If I were to take them to the laundry room, I would find a load of clothes needing to go from the washer to the dryer. Next, I would see the baskets of clean clothes needing to go upstairs. You'd soon find me up in a bedroom folding laundry while my three boxes sat alone back in the family room. As funny as it sounds, the third box will help you keep on task (unless I'm the only person who ever wanders into a room and then forgets the original reason for going there).

For the faint of heart, there is a fourth box. It's a "maybe" box. Put items you aren't sure you are ready to part with in this box. When the box is full, seal it up. Write today's date on the box. Now decide how long you'll keep the box before you donate it. After you've survived without your "maybes" for three or six or nine months or a year, donate the box. (Please do not peek in the box and fall back in love with its precious contents!)

The One-Piece-At-A-Time Method

The next technique is called the piece method. It's a more realistic approach for those of us whose schedules don't allow a large block of time to control clutter. You do one small piece of clutter control at a time, or you use smaller blocks of time, as little as 10 or 15 minutes at a crack. Work on a drawer, a section of cupboard, or part of one closet per day. In a week, a crowded dresser or a messy closet could be in shape.

The As-You-Go Method

My last technique is the as-you-go method. This method helps you get into the habit of donating extra stuff and throwing away any garbage. Weed out stuff as you spy it in your daily rounds at home. For example, when you open your kitchen cupboard tomorrow, count the ceramic mugs inside. Over 20 perhaps? Maybe some match your current dishes, a few are left over from a previously owned set, and several are gifts you received over the years. When was the last time you used all 20? If 20 people came over, wouldn't you probably use disposable cups? Weed out the dustiest five or six in the back immediately by putting them into your donation box.

When you are in your bathroom, toss expired medicines and dated products. In your bedroom, be alert for clothing that isn't being worn, and take it immediately to your donation box. The as-you-go method could quickly become a life habit that helps control clutter on an ongoing basis and it requires little extra time.

Clutter is basically an accumulation of unmade or postponed decisions. We haven't decided where to store things or even whether to keep them, so this stuff just sort of floats around on our tables, counters, and in our crowded closets and drawers. Use the techniques above to become a better clutter decision-maker. This will keep the walls from closing in and free up space, time, and energy for important things.

CHAPTER 9

SIMPLIFIED COOKING

Cooking is fine if I have the time. You'd figure I'd have time in the winter, but I still don't. Who does? Between work, social commitments, appointments, and children's activities, there isn't a lot of room for making delicious home-cooked meals. Frankly, I don't get it. The experts all say the same things: "Plan your meals for a week at a time. Grocery shop once per week at the most. Create a grocery list based on your menu plan. Make your menu plan based on what's in season..."

Yeah, right... in a perfect world. How do I know on Monday what I'll want to eat on Thursday? For that matter, how do I know who will be there to eat it with me if I bother to cook it? It is hard in real life to do what the experts suggest. So, here are a few simple thoughts that help me cook.

Try the 8am rule (or whatever time suits you depending on when you regularly leave your house for the day)

I try to decide by 8am what we will have for dinner that night. This is a load off my mind for the rest of the day. Deciding is sometimes harder than cooking. I have the mental energy in the morning to plan a meal. If I don't make a plan and 6 pm rolls around, our delicious home-cooked dinner is merely an unformed blob in my brain and a frozen lump of whatever somewhere in my freezer. With the 8am rule, I don't have to stand in my kitchen at 6pm — tired, hungry and undecided. Besides, my tired and hungry family is usually standing next to me by then, and they want to eat now! When I decide what's for dinner in the morning, I have options. If I need an ingredient, I might have time during the day or on the way home from work to get it. If I need to thaw something out, I have time.

Don't throw out that old crock-pot. Don't laugh. Go and dig out that crock-pot and the little recipe booklet that came with it. Expand your crock-pot repertoire. There are many, many crock-pot cookbooks at secondhand book stores and garage sales. It's so simple. Ingredients go into the pot in the morning, and dinner comes out that night! And the crook pot makes the house smell like someone (maybe even me) has been slaving away in the kitchen all day.

Check out the simple cookbooks. I admit it. I like to read cookbooks more than I like to cook. That said, there are several kinds of helpful books out there. Keep looking until you find one that fits your own style. I suggest checking them out from the library – try them before buying them.

Sometimes a cookbook author uses ingredients or cooking techniques you don't care for. Or you discover your version of a stocked pantry is so different from the author's that the cookbook isn't a good fit. If the author thinks canned artichokes or hearts of palm are pantry items, I know I need to look elsewhere.

Cookbooks usually clue you in to their nature with their titles. There are make-ahead cookbooks, crock-pot cookbooks, few-ingredient cookbooks, make-it-fast cookbooks, make-it-fast-and-with-fewer-ingredient cookbooks, frugal cookbooks, cooking technique books, and menus-planned-for-you cookbooks:

- With make-ahead cookbooks, cook less often. These books show you how to have a couple weeks or a month's worth of dinners ready in your freezer:

  Once-A-Month Cooking by Mimi Wilson and Beth Lagerborg

  Frozen Assets: How to cook for a day and eat for a month by Deborah Taylor-Hough, and *Dinner's in the Freezer* by Jill Bond

- Let your crock-pot do the cooking for you. It won't heat up your kitchen, and your home will smell great:

Rival Crock-Pot Cooking

The 150 Best Slow Cooker Recipes by Judith Finlayson – which has photographs and says which dishes can even be assembled the night before and refrigerated overnight

The Ultimate Slow Cooker Cookbook by Carol Heding Munson – with helpful photos and nutritional information per serving

Slow Cookers for Dummies by Tom Lacalamita and Glenna Vance – which tells me this is an "in" way to cook since a slow cooker cookbook has made it into this series of popular reference books

America's Best Slow Cooker Recipes by Donna-Marie Pye – which includes tips, menu suggestions and make-ahead options

Fix-It and Forget-It Cookbook by Dawn Ranck and Phyllis Pellman Good – which has more than 800 recipes from cooks all around the USA

- Cook with fewer ingredients. Cookbooks for this usually tell you so in their titles,

  Recipes 1-2-3: fabulous food using only three ingredients by Rozanne Gold

  6-Ingredients or Less Cookbook by Carlean Johnson

- Cook faster. These books often promise speed in their titles:

  20 Minute Menus by Marian Burros

- Cook faster and with fewer ingredients. A favorite of mine is

  Desperation Dinners by Beverly Mills and Alicia Ross

  The Minimalist Cooks Dinner by Mark Bittman

- Cook frugally with

  365 Quick, Easy, & Inexpensive Menus, by Penny Stone

- Cook by learning from a technique book that will show you how to cook whatever ingredients you have on hand:

  How to Cook Without a Book: Recipes and Techniques Every

Cook Should Know by Heart by Pam Anderson
- Cook but let someone else plan the grocery shopping and menu for you:

   Saving Dinner: The Menus, Recipes, and Shopping Lists to Bring Your Family Back to the Table by Leanne Ely. Ely has published several books geared toward different kinds of eating choices.

Finally, consider an alternative food pyramid. My children have been taught the nutritional pyramid with fats at the top and grains at the bottom.

This is a different version. The pinnacle of success, at the top of the pyramid, is the goal of a home cooked meal. At the bottom of the pyramid is the ultimate fallback — taking my family out to eat at a restaurant. I forget the many things in-between. Sometimes, if I can't reach the top of this pyramid, I slide right down to the bottom. However, there really are other options on the way down to slow or stop my fall.

Going from top to bottom, the pyramid might look like this:

A made-from-scratch home-cooked meal would be at the top. Next, there could be a home-cooked meal that uses some prepared ingredients like a jar of spaghetti sauce. Below that could be a small easy breakfast-style meal like pancakes or eggs. Further down could be a meal-in-a-box or a frozen family dinner. Below that, a fairly frugal frozen pizza or "TV dinner" supplemented with fresh fruit, vegetables, and beverages on hand at home. Closer to the bottom is a more-expensive take-out or delivered dinner supplemented with the home items mentioned before. Finally, at the bottom of the pyramid, is simply going out to a restaurant, which will probably be less healthy, and take more money and time than I want to spend.

Catch yourself before you slide to the bottom of the pyramid. You might enjoy exploring some less expensive and more healthful choices between the top and the bottom of the pyramid when you don't have time to totally cook from scratch.

Don't be plagued by the guilt of home-cooked meals that look like the cover of a magazine or something you saw on television. The notion of home-cooked meals is deeply hooked into our internal "should's" and "ought to's." Let go of the illusion. The best way to simplify cooking is to recognize your own reality. Simplify your pantry and your cooking style to fit your life. It will be worth the effort and it will result in meals that work for your life style.

CHAPTER 10

SADLY SORTING SOCKS
& SOLVING LAUNDRY WOES

Are you tired of doing the laundry dance or do you delight in doing it? Perhaps the drudgery and repetition of this common task wear you down, or do you love the smell of clean clothes fresh from the dryer and enjoy the calming mood induced by sorting clothes and putting them away?

If you are not happy with the laundry dance and you hate to fold or to put away (these are actually two different "issues" which call for two different solutions), then here is how to simplify each process.

Hate to fold? Folding clothes can be a repetitive boring task, so any way to speed up the process can help. I find sorting socks to be a major player here — you know, the large white mound of halfway turned inside-out nuggets heaped on my bed that I've vowed to finish before I crawl into bed.

Many laundry "experts" have told me the same "solution": Train family members to pin their socks together before laundering. Ha!

There are simpler ideas. Buy a different sock brand or style for each person in the family so you can sort them quickly. When that isn't possible, for example, all little white anklet socks look pretty much the same, what then? How can you tell if that tiny white sock is really little sister's sock, or if it is big sister's sock that has lingered in the dryer too long? I don't care to stand pondering these weighty matters at 11pm! If you like to sew, put a different color stitch on the toe of each sibling's sock. Pick one color for each person and stick with it. I am lazy. I make a dot on each sock toe with a permanent marker. Markers come in many colors.

Another sock option is to keep two mesh laundry bags in each person's sock drawer. Use one bag for clean socks and the other bag for dirty ones. Dirty sock bags are gathered weekly and washed, leaving the socks in the bags throughout the process. After being laundered, clean socks are transferred to the clean sock bag in each person's drawer. Family members are responsible for finding matched pairs in their bags when they need them and putting dirty socks in their dirty sock bag.

General Laundry Sorting & Folding Solutions

If you have a large family, consider eliminating sorting. Some large families simply do laundry by person rather than by type of laundry. This eliminates sorting by person all together. Marking clothing, using mesh bags, and laundering by person are techniques that work for T-shirts, underwear, and other laundry too.

A way to reduce laundry-folding repetition is to do it less often. Give yourself a longer break between sessions by borrowing a trick from our mothers or grandmothers: Pick a laundry day and do laundry only once per week. Make this day known to other family members so they know when they can get things washed. If a teenager has a problem with this, just say "No" – or better yet, say "do it yourself!"

If you have children, delegate folding. Long before I was fully comfortable with children running electrical kitchen gadgets, they folded laundry for me.

Finally, some people don't mind folding laundry at all. They find it relaxing or they catch up on a television series by watching a taped show, or they chat with a friend on the phone while they work. So, consider simply reframing how you view this task in your own mind.

What Do We Have To Do After the Laundry is Folded?

Putting folded laundry away is sometimes what frustrates

people. They have nice clean neat stacks of laundry waiting in laundry baskets, stacked on the table, piled on a chair, down on the floor, or waiting by the stairs to go up to the bedrooms. Of course, these piles only stay neat and clean until some poor partially clothed soul comes along to dig through them to find what they need. Does this sound like your situation? Why does this happen? Maybe it just isn't fun to put nice neat clean clothing into jumbled up or overcrowded drawers and closets?

Weed out to conquer
Simplify putting laundry away by keeping closets and drawers clutter-free and organized. Regularly weed out clothing that isn't being used. Strictly speaking, if you do laundry weekly, you wouldn't need more than seven pairs of anything. The exception is the need to change clothing for activities like sports and exercise.

Toss mismatches, extras, things that are so worn that they are never worn, and what you and others never wear because it isn't liked. Styles don't come back quite the same, and if you don't like something today, you probably won't like it tomorrow. Free yourself today from extraneous laundry clutter that simply crams and wrinkles the things your family really wants to wear.

Divide to conquer
Install drawer dividers to divide and conquer drawers. Drawer dividers can be as easy and simple as cardboard boxes cut to size. Dividing drawers keeps drawers from looking like they've been stirred up with a spoon. It provides great visual organization that is easy to maintain. Dividing space also helps quickly clue you in on when it is time to weed out a clothing category: If the sock section of the drawer is overflowing, it is time to weed out socks!

Delegate to conquer
Another way to simplify putting laundry away is to assign the

task to others. Make each family member responsible for putting away his or her own laundry. If the drawers look like they've been stirred with a spoon but you don't have to look in them anymore, are they still stirred up?

CHAPTER 11

TOY CLUTTER AFTER THE CHRISTMAS HOLIDAYS

My friend Mary called me after the holidays. "Well, have you found the floor yet?" she said. She has young children too. I knew what she meant. After numerous gifts from well-meaning friends and family, my kids had received so many new toys. And it wasn't as if there was a toy shortage at our home before the holidays. The floor can disappear under this generosity. What parent hasn't, at least once, been seized by the urge to take a shovel and a garbage bag into their children's rooms and go for it?

Winter is also the season when the walls shrink inward. So rather than label toy clutter as hopeless, I choose a frontal attack (minus the shovel). The first step is to reduce the sheer quantity of toys. It helps to weed out toys regularly (every six months or so). Now I know you are saying, "Easier said than done," but please hang in there for a moment.

A Reason To Reduce

My experience with my eldest child taught me that fewer toys works better for some children. When it came to sitting down to play creatively for an extended period of time with a toy, less was definitely more in her case. The fewer toys I had in her room to distract her, the better she played with those she had. Try fewer toys if you've observed "toy dumping" or lack of focus while playing.

Reclaim rooms

One friend of mine limits where toys may live. She reclaimed her

40

family room as a multi-purpose room. Toys are brought in for play. But, as a general rule, they go back to each child's room for storage purposes. I also don't think it is cruel or unusual punishment to reclaim an adult space in part of the home. Maybe the living room and dining room can be designated as "toy free" zones.

Beware of duplicates

Don't double (or triple) up on toys. My second child taught me not to duplicate function with toys. Between gifts and hand-me-downs from her sister, duplications sometimes happened. As an infant, she wound up with six standard pop-up toys in assorted makes and models. Of course I wanted her to develop her infant motor skills. But we didn't need six toys that basically worked the same way.

I began to look at blocks and markers this way. How many "different" building sets (plastic blocks, wooden blocks, plastic logs, foam blocks...) did my children really require in order to become budding architects? How many different markers (over-writers, under-writers, fine-line, wide-line, neons, fluorescents, classics...) did they "need" to develop their artistic talents?

Rotate out toys

Another trick to reduce toy clutter is to rotate out some toys for a while. Put unused toys in a rotation box. Bring them back out on a sick day or a snow day. A stricter version is to have a "time out" box for toys that haven't been picked up after a reasonable request or specified time. A mom in one of my classes said she sends any toys that aren't back in their rightful places after clean-up time "to jail."

Talk

When weeding out toys, it is helpful to get input from your children too. They may surprise you and be more willing to part with things than you would have guessed. They may even enjoy the decision-making process. As for young children, we sometimes give them too much to manage and organize. Could you tidy a major department store by yourself?

Motivate hoarders

If you have a "saver" or hoarder in the family, there are other options: You can limit the space they have to store their treasures. Give them a certain number of shelves or boxes for their collections. Or, you can offer an incentive. Let them sell their extras to a secondhand store and spend the proceeds at a store of their choice. With pennies on the dollar being returned for a typical transaction, you will still come out ahead space-wise.

Enjoy!

When toys are weeded down to a reasonable quantity, it is easier to find a functional place to organize and store them. The kids can get to the toys they want more easily, and it will be easier to pick up. Weeding out toys isn't a goal in itself. It is a tool to teach children useful life management skills and to reclaim valuable energy and space in a busy family's life.

Besides, life is too short to spend it sorting all those puzzle and game pieces back into the right boxes. Right?

CHAPTER 12

LIVING ROOM OR FAMILY ROOM: ORGANIZE OUR WINTER HABITAT

Aside from the fact that many of us hang out in the kitchen and dump our stuff in there, what other room do you and yours hang out in when post-holiday calm and winter blahs set in? The living room or the family room, perhaps? Whichever room, do you feel some days that it could just be dubbed the messy room? How was it looking after television football on Sunday? Whichever room people "live in" in your home, pick up some tips to simplify this high-use winter family habitat.

Sometimes our "family" room holds more stuff than family: remote controls, videos, CDs, books, newspapers, games, hobbies, slippers, blankets, stuffed animals, coffee cups, and whatever else everyone in my family happened to be holding in their hands when they walked into the room. Aarrgh!

I am glad my family has a winter hangout, and I wouldn't even want to change their habits of using it (much). I think the techniques we use to organize and simplify whatever room we're talking about could fit the people who live there. Perfect people don't live here. We do!

Weed Out

Since my family seems to constantly add to the clutter in our family room, I try to weed out any excess clutter in the room itself. With books, CDs, DVDs, and other things already sitting around, I don't need to overdress this spot with decorating knick-knacks too.

After the holidays is also a good time to donate books, magazines, videos, and anything else your family may have outgrown or replaced at Christmas. Keep in mind the famous "one in, one out" rule. If you received a new book, maybe it is time to pass on an old one...

Remove Excess furniture

Eliminate or store excess furniture or decorating if you can. Years ago, after observing the open living room floor space at our day care provider's home, I went home and eliminated our living room coffee table! (Okay, I stored it.) Before you shake your head, consider this: Getting rid of the coffee table reduced the heavy dirt and carpet wear pattern on the floor around it. It also made more room for my children to roll around safely on the floor and play. They won't always be young, but right now not having a coffee table is a good fit for my family's style.

Clever Containers

I am also in love with "containerizing" everything that can be contained. Piles of stuff sitting around can look messy. Stuff in containers looks calm, and neat to my eye. I'm picky here. I want the containers in the family room to be functional and to look nice there too!

When we're talking about furniture, I like enclosed entertainment centers and barrister-style bookcases — because I don't have to look at all the little stuff or dust the open shelves all the time either. Wicker baskets are great too. They can hold anything from slippers or blankets to books, magazines, or craft projects.

Larger boxed games and puzzles can be problematic because of their size, but they can also be stored near where they are used. Try a large wicker or plastic laundry basket, or use the space underneath a couch or loveseat, or add some shelving to a closet or base cabinet to store them.

In addition to baskets, I sometimes use nice large canvas bags to hold library books or a temporary project that I want to keep in the room. A sturdy canvas bag is multi-purpose because I can just grab it when it is time to take our library books back, and it looks better to have our library books in a bag next to the end table instead of piled on top of the table. I even choose bags in colors that match the rooms they live in.

A Place For Everything

If there are "homes" in the family room for stuff people use, it will make it easier for everyone to help keep things picked up. Sometimes things don't get picked up because no one is sure where this stuff could go, or there isn't any room left where these things are supposed to go. This is why periodically weeding out is important—unless you want to keep getting bigger containers and eventually bigger houses just to hold your stuff!

Maintenance

After removing clutter and organizing the remainder into functional containers, there is maintenance. To keep a semblance of order in a high-use room, help family members get into the habit of taking something with them every time they leave the room. This will help "things" find their way back to their proper storage locations.

Another trick is to spend five minutes straightening up the family room every night for a week. You will be surprised by the improvement. Set a kitchen timer. Don't skip a night, but also don't let five minutes expand into 30 – then you know you've stayed up too late and you won't be inclined to clean up before bedtime again. It is amazing what can be done in five minutes per night. Try it before you laugh!

I like to nest in the winter. It is a joy to burrow into the family room with my family for an evening or a Sunday afternoon. Purge the excess clutter, make homes for things your family enjoys using there, and maintain the room to make it a comfortable winter habitat for everyone.

CHAPTER 13

CLUTTER & CLEANING PRODUCTS!

Sometimes just updating my cleaning products motivates me to do a better job on housework, for a while anyway. I'm also a guppy for new technology, and technology does change. Let's come clean (pun intended) about what works. Here are the results of my recent cleaning product shopping and home trials.

Household wet wipes for bathroom and kitchen swiping. Who'd have thought? Last time I checked, I thought wet wipes were for cleaning baby. I thought wrong. Though a little costly, I can keep a container in each bathroom to give it a quick wipe every once in a while. I am more inclined to keep up on bathroom grime because I don't have to run to the basement for a mop and a bucket.

One of the new products I tried didn't work out. The product, which promised easy cleaning and better breathing, still had an odor and it didn't seem to do a better job than the bathroom spray that I had used for years. I could have saved myself money and time by checking out the product review (only 3 out of 5 stars) at www.epinions.com. Oh well. Live and learn.

How about those disposable dust wipes you can use to dust anywhere in the home? They seem a little expensive, but after wiping off all blades of all the ceiling fans in our home that had run continuously all summer, I was ecstatic to throw that grime away rather than run it through my laundry.

In the winter, windows are closed. This has me thinking about household odors. I've discovered the spray-on fabric deodor-izers. They really work! I was able to get all of the cigarette odor out of a used sleeper sofa I purchased. I also found that it worked great on clothing in closets and upholstered furnishings.

Whatever the product's composition is, chemically speaking, it seems to eliminate rather than just mask odor.

If you get really interested in cleaning products, Don Aslett, well-known cleaning and clutter control author, has a catalog for professional and household cleaners. I like looking in his catalog periodically to see what he thinks are the latest and greatest products. He's right on target with microfiber cleaning cloths. To get a copy of his catalog, call 1-800-451-2402 or check out his website at www.cleanreport.com.

After my research and home trials, I decided it is worth it to check the catalogs and cleaning product aisles now and again because some things have been improved upon and because it is fun to have new toys to help me stay motivated to do these tedious tasks.

I also wondered why, in casual conversation, these tasks are rarely discussed. Why is it taboo to ask someone how they dust their home or clean their toilet or wash their clothes? After all, we all have to do this stuff, and maybe if we put our heads together more often, we could simplify our lives by using better products and methods.

CHAPTER 14

AIR CLUTTER: A BREATH OF FRESH AIR

Sometimes my house stinks. No, I'm not talking about my floor plan, limited square footage, or even my spouse, children, or the muddy footed dogs that constantly tromp in and out. I'm talking about that first breath of stagnant, stale air that I inhale when I step inside my door this time of year. Odor clutter.

There's no place like home, and no place smells quite like home. If you stop to think about it, each home actually has its own unique scent — kind of like a signature. If that's the case, I'm not sure I like my home's handwriting, especially at this time of year. Even in a mild winter, enclosed dwelling air can still stink.

I used to run around my house with a spray can of air freshener before I was expecting company. I figured there had to be some better options out there. Over the years, I found other things that worked better to freshen up our winter dwelling.

Change the furnace filter every six months or more often if it is a thinner filter. Consider setting the blower fan on the furnace to run continuously, even when the furnace isn't running to heat your home. Constantly running the fan will reduce household dust, filter out odors, and even out any temperature and humidity differences throughout your home.

Put a scented dryer sheet in your vacuum bag the next time you change the bag. It will reduce any stale odors that escape from your vacuum when you clean. Along the same lines, change the vacuum bag once or twice per month — even if it is only half-full. You will vacuum more efficiently because of improved airflow, and your home will smell better.

If you own a vacuum with a HEPA filter, dust first and then vacuum because dusting can stir up dirt and knock it to the floor.

If you own an older vacuum, consider vacuuming first and then dusting to wipe up whatever gets blown out of the vacuum cleaner. In either case, check out the new disposable electrostatic dust wipes. They're great for computers, televisions, and electronic equipment, and they catch the dust rather than just push it around.

Wash interior entry mats. Though this may seem obvious, don't over look them. (You do own the washable ones right?) These mats pick up all the damp dirt and gunk that get tracked in on the bottoms of shoes and boots. Sometimes that stale odor I catch as I step into my house is simply dirty entryway mats.

Try placing odor eliminators in any stale closets, and basement or laundry areas. I try to look for plug-ins, stick-ups, or freestanding units that claim to eliminate odors rather than just mask them. Ask a realtor what they use or check at your local hardware store.

Do some washing. If the coat closet smells stale, it may be time to wash everyone's coats. If a bedroom closet doesn't smell great, it may be time to launder or dry clean items in there too. Wash rugs, towels, and bedding regularly. This will help track down and eliminate some of those miscellaneous odor generators.

If you own an upright vacuum or a small portable canister that came with any specialty tools, spend a couple of hours playing with just those gadgets. I'm talking about the crevice tool, the edger, the wand, and the upholstery attachment. Instead of intermittently using these tools as you do your regular vacuuming, resolve to spend a block of time specifically tackling window treatments, cold air returns, upholstery, base moldings, crevices, light fixtures, and other hard to reach spots in each room of your home. You know the places I'm talking about. Give yourself two hours to specifically tackle the hidden tough spots. Doing it this way is easier and more thorough than trying to switch back and forth to these tools while doing the regular vacuuming. Your house will be cleaner and fresher for your efforts.

Open the windows. So what if it is cold outside! Open the windows for a brief period once per week or so. Set the kitchen timer for ten minutes. It doesn't take long. The best cure for stale air is fresh air, the real thing.

When all else fails and you find yourself in need of a simple breath of fresh air, bundle up, put on nonskid shoes or boots, and take a walk. After all, some of us are Minnesotans!

CHAPTER 15

WHAT ABOUT INHERITED CLUTTER?

Have you ever inherited or been gifted with stuff? If you feel like you are "stuffocating" (suffocating from all of your stuff — a new word that came up at my local simple living group meeting), what can you do with all the stuff you've received? How do you decide what to do with Grandma and Grandpa's stuff or Mom and Dad's stuff, all those well-intentioned gifts, hand-me-downs, or things you are hanging onto for someone else? There are several approaches to help deal with the bounty many of us have received.

Memories
First, keep in mind that you keep the memory of a person alive in your heart, not in the boxes of stuff from them that are sitting in your basement. Keep a couple representative pieces rather than whole collections. One or two extra special mementos can remind you of a person and be more meaningful than excess boxes of plain old stuff.

Tell
Don't store memories. Display them! Frame Grandma's hand crocheted doily and hang it in a place of honor in your home. It is also very important to write the story down on the backside of the frame to help keep her story alive. Tell your children, guests, and anyone else who will listen about Grandma.

Don't Keep Misery
Remember that people give each other things as acts of kindness. No one intends to add to someone else's clutter misery.

Appreciate the intent of gifts and inherited items but feel free to sell, donate, or re-gift items to others who might have more appreciation for them.

Items can be sold in the newspaper, on the Internet at craigslist.org or on www.ebay.com or by local estate sale or auction companies who will buy stuff outright or take it on consignment. Check the yellow pages, and feel free to get more than one opinion on values.

Other People's Clutter

Clutter boundaries: Don't let anyone else's clutter drag you down. If people try to get you to store their stuff, it is fine to be generous with your space on a short-term basis. Establish a specific deadline for them to retrieve the item. Remind them once. And, finally, feel free to dispose of this stuff as you see fit after the deadline has come and gone. What am I saying here? Parents, you are not responsible for indefinitely storing stuff for your grown children. It isn't fair or respectful to you. And, also, do not "gift" stuff to your grown children with strings attached. It isn't really a gift when you are basically asking for free storage under the "loving" guise of "keeping it in the family!"

Give Respectfully

What about our own giving? Many have heard the biblical quote, "It is better to give than to receive." Many of us heard it as children when our parents tried to instill a generous spirit in us and teach us to share. In that context, it seemed better to give than to receive for moral and ethical reasons rather than for personal reasons.

We can give generously to get rid of clutter. It allows us to get rid of extra physical stuff, as well as the emotional, and spiritual baggage that clings to our possessions. We get a feeling of satisfaction for sharing our excess with others. At the same time, we free ourselves from the weight of our clutter. Give respectfully, however, by giving to those who can actually use the items they receive. Do not dump on a fellow clutter bug because you know they have a weakness for stuff. It isn't kind, and you aren't doing them any favors.

If you are passing items down in your family, remember to pass down the stories too. Write down why these items have monetary or sentimental value. If you don't, the treasures may get tossed with the trash. Also, it is kinder to specify who gets what today to prevent painful arguments after you are gone.

Wait!

Now, getting rid of clutter has not been about getting rid of everything. The general rules are to keep what is beautiful, useful, and sentimental. Or, as you weed out, simply look at something and go with your gut response to it before your well-intentioned rationalizations kick in — you know, "It was a gift," or "It was Grandma's," or "I paid good money for it..." If your gut just doesn't like it, get rid of it! Life brings us enough stress without hanging onto items that increase stress. Period.

CHAPTER 16

UNCLUTTERED ORGANIZATION MEANS FUNCTIONAL STORAGE CONTAINERS

After household clutter is cleared out, the next step for simple living is to organize the stuff that's left. In theory, everything that is left will be stuff that is liked and used regularly. That means this stuff must be easy to reach. Planning, location, and design of storage containers can be considered to avoid frustration.

Plan ahead

Measure and figure out your storage needs before you buy a nifty storage container. Do a final clutter clearance too! We accumulated many videos over the years. Next, we bought CDs. Now we also accumulate DVDs. Before we could get an organizer for all of it, we needed to do some final purging, then counting and finally shopping research on the Internet.

Allow grow room

We also had to make an educated guess about our videos and DVDs to figure out how much future grow room we wanted to design into our storage system. Most of us will continue to acquire more — whatever it is. Make allowances for this on the front end and be happier in the long run.

Location

Location. Location. Location. Ask yourself if the storage container is handy. It might appear simple, but it may not be functional. We had piles of CDs tucked in an end table cabinet. It made the room look tidy, but it was hard to read all the CD titles and reach them. We ended up with a storage rack that stands on the floor. For the first time, we can organize the CDs and read all the titles at once! A simple life is a functional life, not necessarily a perfectly tidy life.

Where is the easiest location for you to use a storage container? Is it easy? Is it fun? If it isn't, you won't go there! Let me tell you about my houseplant fertilizer. For a long time, my five-pound plastic bag of this stuff lived in its original cardboard box out in the garage. Eventually, it got closer to my houseplants by making its way down to my laundry room. Since my watering can lived under my kitchen sink and all my plants were upstairs, I still was in a situation where I'd think about fertilizing my houseplants, but I wouldn't feel like running downstairs to dig out the fertilizer. To remedy this, I finally realized the fertilizer belonged under my kitchen sink, next to my watering can.

Design for convenience

Storage container design is also important. Does the container itself work? Are you willing to get stuff out of the container when you need to? Or, does the container you've chosen put you off? Now that my fertilizer was next to the watering can, I found I still wasn't fertilizing my houseplants because I didn't like the leaky plastic bag inside the disintegrating cardboard box. When I used it, I didn't like sticking a regular kitchen spoon into the bag or getting plant fertilizer scattered all over my kitchen counter top.

The answer for me was to pour the fertilizer into an empty plastic peanut butter jar, label it, and plunk an old baby spoon inside the jar with the fertilizer. Wow! I'm looking forward to the next time it is time for me to fertilize houseplants.

Here is a tip. Large-mouth containers, ranging in size from empty frosting containers to large plastic ice-cream pails are great for anything you need to scoop out and measure – baking soda, baking powder, flour, sugar... Much less winds up spilled on the counter when you use it. Be sure to label and date everything!

Design is key. The design must fit your application. Smaller toiletries slipping between the wires of a white wire storage basket was a daily frustration until I replaced it with a solid plastic container. Plastic versus cardboard matters too if you are storing liquids that could run down the sides of their containers or leak, and you want to protect the surface they sit on.

You probably already have your plant fertilizer near your watering can, but pay attention to yourself. When do you neglect or stall about doing something because it isn't convenient? When you feel your frustration rise, look at the location and design that you have and change it to make your storage containers work for you!

CHAPTER 17

SEEK HELP FOR LIFE CLUTTER

Give. Give. Give. We work hard giving every day. We give at our jobs, and for our families, and for other obligations that life throws at us. But, help? How often do you ask for help? Do you just decide you don't deserve help? Do you figure you'd probably be turned down if you did ask for help? Or, maybe, you're trying for martyrdom? Do you usually just decide it's just better (perfectionism) if you do it all yourself?

Are you tired? Worn out? Frustrated? "Maxed" out? Are you constantly pouring all your energy out for others? If you want to simplify your life, it involves more than clutter control and household organizing. To simplify your life, you need to be willing to ask for help.

Ouch! If I have to ask for help, I'm a failure. I'm supposed to be able to manage everything by myself. Really? How many perfectly balanced accomplished lives do you see out there? How many times have you peeked into other people lives and thought to yourself that he or she could get some help with this thing or that? You are not a failure if you ask for help. You are a problem solver. Would you feel guilty if you asked for help? Asking for help is an act of kindness to ourselves. It isn't wrong to be kind to ourselves. Really! Now, why is there still all this guilt at the thought of asking for help? I suppose we don't want to be thought of as selfish, but think about this for a minute.

If we aren't kind to ourselves, who will be? We are members of a society where people increasingly complain about poor service, rude drivers, and other impolite behavior. Maybe we're harsh toward other people because we have become so harsh toward ourselves. Maybe if more of us learned to be kinder to ourselves and to ask for help when we need it, we'd have more energy left over for greater kindness and better service to others.

When you ask for help, you will usually get help. It's true! Most people, most of the time, want to help and enjoy being helpful. People will help if they can.

I was in awe of another mom who recently asked for help. She had two children in two different music classrooms at the same time every Saturday. It was smart time management because she only had to make the drive across town once per week instead of twice. The rub was that a parent was supposed to be with each child during their classes to help them. At first the mom ran back and forth from room to room. She and her children quickly became frustrated.

To solve this problem, she asked for help. She asked a mom, whose daughter was further along in the music program, if her daughter could sit in with one of her children each week. The parent of the helper daughter was happy to "loan" her out because she had another child in a sports activity at the same time. The daughter enjoyed being a "teacher," and the music mom no longer had to run back and forth between the classrooms. It turned out to be a simple solution where everyone won because one person was willing to ask for help.

We've all heard that "It is better to give than to receive." We can't have it all or do it all ourselves. Life is too complicated. Simplify your life and help those around you in unanticipated ways by remembering to take turns being on both sides of the equation. Be willing to ask for help and to give it.

CHAPTER 18

WANT TO MAKE CHANGES? FIRST, GET "UNSTUCK"

Several weeks into the new year, how are those New Year's resolutions going? Every year, around this time, many of us try to change some aspect of our lives. The holidays are over, winter has set in, and maybe we have time to reflect on our life. Sadly, we sometimes make the same resolutions for change year after year: We vow to lose weight, get organized, save money...

We know what we're "supposed" to do. We've heard it all before. Why is it so hard to break old habits and to make changes? Why do we often stay stuck year after year? How can we get "unstuck?" Who could help? Family? Friends? Who?

Maybe a life coach could help. It is one option to help people get "unstuck" with life goals. I visited several times with a personal coach. She says therapy looks into your past, but personal coaching looks toward your future. She says a coach will work around your personal "gremlins" rather than try to resolve them or argue with them. I was intrigued.

What is the difference between coaching and therapy? A therapist is trained to deal with psychological issues and family of origin stuff. Digging into the past may be an important thing to do, but it might be a long road to achieve current life goals.

Why not get support for change from a family member? A family member may be too close or too kind to be objective. A coach is not a family member. Or, how about help from a caring friend? A friend is great for empathy and emotional support, but again, a friend might choose to be more kind than honest. We are all grateful for family and friends. They care about us and support us, but they may not know how to guide us or keep us on track.

A personal coach works with a client to establish goals and then helps the client stay on track to achieve those goals. To me, it sounds like coaching may be a way to get specific advice from someone who would be objective. It also provides accountability. Someone will be checking on you! And, due to its very nature, coaching is a confidential relationship.

Many coaches have had formal training. Some have trained with the California-based Coaches Training Institute. It would be wise to ask a potential coach what their training, experience, and expertise in coaching is. It is your money. Look for someone who is going to be a fit for you.

I learned that some coaches would offer a free 30-minute introductory session. Phone and email may do much of the work after that. Coaches may have specific specialties. The coach I spoke to focuses on parenting but coaches on other topics too.

For more information on coaching, check out www.CoachFederation.org, which is the website of the International Coach Federation out of Washington, D.C. You can search there for a coach that is a match on a variety of different criteria.

If goal-setting techniques aren't working to help you toward your goals, there are other possibilities to successfully achieve New Year's resolutions. Simple living is about trimming off the excess, focusing on personal priorities, and finding personal balance in a chaotic world. Personal coaching might be one more avenue to try to break old habits and focus on priorities.

CHAPTER 19

WHATEVER YOU DO, DON'T QUIT: "JUST KEEP SWIMMING"

In the Disney movie *Finding Nemo* there is a little fish named Dory with a short-term memory problem. Can anyone else out there relate? To stay calm and keep going in spite of the forgetfulness that sometimes makes the world a very frightening place, Dory regularly chants, "Just keep swimming. Just keep swimming. Just keep swimming, swimming, swimming." Dory is absolutely right.

At a time when New Year's resolutions fade, winter seems to drag on forever, and weight loss isn't going as well as I want it to, I think of Dory and many others like her. Is your clutter weighing you down? Though it would be nice to be naturally slender, smart, quick, talented, or well organized, that isn't the answer. The real solution to life's frustrations isn't a solution. It is a process and it requires only one thing—persistence.

I often seem to be working on body clutter. The first few pounds came off pretty easily, but then it became more difficult. In fact, there have been some weeks when I have gained weight rather than lost it. When that happened, I became frustrated which simply led to more eating (substitute consumption if you're thinking clutter here). When I haven't been successful, I've just wanted to quit. Then it hit me, the point to getting rid of weight or clutter, isn't to "be the best," it is just to do it. "Just keep swimming. Just keep swimming, swimming, swimming."

I won't be able to say I lost a lot of body clutter in record time. In fact, I am behind schedule and my original goal may not be realistic, but that isn't the point.

To achieve success, I simply have to stick with it. I have to be persistent. I have to keep recommitting. The same thought applies to household clutter. We don't have to make our homes perfect in a weekend. Most of us probably couldn't do that anyway. What we can do is to recognize that clutter clearing is a process and that things will improve if we simply continue to stick with it little by little.

One book that helps me to stay on task in many areas of my life is Rick Warren's New York Times bestseller *The Purpose Driven Life – What On Earth Am I Here For?*

He says since moods and emotions can fluctuate frequently, we would be wise not to base our long-term beliefs, decisions, and life behaviors on them. Rick Warren states that if we know God's purpose for us, then decisions become simplified, stress is reduced, and we can achieve greater focus in our lives.

In spite of trying to practice voluntary simplicity, I am great at getting distracted. The ideas in Warren's book help me to remember to regularly ask myself if my thoughts, words, and deeds are matching my long-term priorities.

My 99-year-old grandpa phrased it another way, "It doesn't matter if you lose the battle; you want to win the war. In fact, you can lose every battle, and it doesn't matter, as long as you win the war." He was talking about this in the context of creating a successful marriage, but I think it can apply to all relationships and virtually everything else in life, including dealing with clutter or weight loss.

It is okay to momentarily quit. It is realistic and human to have lapses. The point is that we have to pick ourselves or our clutter back up again and continue. Don't quit when the piles reappear on the kitchen counter or the table disappears under the tax paperwork. Keep whittling away at it and you will succeed!

CHAPTER 20

PEOPLE CLUTTER?

People clutter. We all have it. We might not want to admit it. It isn't a popular thing to discuss. How can we strengthen relationships we value and move on from relationships that drain us? Would it be worth it to clear some people clutter from our lives? After all, it might be awkward, painful, and certainly not "nice".

I am not a people expert, but I have definite opinions when I think about simple living and the people in my life.

Reality check: We each have a finite amount of time, so we can only do a reasonable job maintaining a finite number of relationships. Most of us don't choose to make the time to have coffee dates or social activities seven days per week! When we do make time to get close to people, we could choose to connect with the people who matter most to us.

Is that an ugly thing to say? I'm not saying we can't be friendly and civil to the rest of the world!

Who matters? I have been thinking about three kinds of relationships in our lives: good, bad, and required. We have special friends we can share anything with and who we wouldn't trade for the world. We have bad relationships that we may be keeping out of habit – relationships that may even be holding us back in our lives. Finally, we have the relationships we were born into. We didn't choose our parents, children, or other relatives, yet they are part of our lives.

Strengthen the positive relationships. Don't let go. Make it a habit to see these people regularly. Make it a habit to tell these people how you feel about them. I enjoy having a coffee date every two weeks with a dear friend of 20 years. We've had this standing coffee date for many years. We may or may not continue depending on how it fits into each of our futures, but for now, we're both enjoying the regular contact.

Work on required relationships. If there is a problem situation, spend more time on it rather than less time. I once knew a woman who was having trouble with one of her daughters. The daughter was getting into trouble and becoming more and more difficult to interact with. Though there may have been a temptation to take the easy road and avoid the situation, the mother chose instead to spend extra time with this child. Rather than run away, she chose to work on the situation and things with her daughter eventually improved.

Finally, there are bad relationships or ones that have gone stale. Careers, hobbies, and even certain people may have been a fit for who we were at a certain time or life stage. Can these relationships be repaired? Maybe. I checked www.amazon.com and got 32,000 hits for books that address relationships. There is help out there now for almost every situation. (Where were those books when I was a teenager and young adult? Though, maybe that didn't matter if I wasn't ready yet to hear what these books had to say...)

If a bad relationship can't be repaired, think about making a tough decision. Don't be afraid to move on from bad or stale relationships. Life is too short. In fact, you will be acting with integrity, which, in the long run, will help the other person too.

Moving on from a relationship, if that is what is needed, creates room for new people we are interested in bringing into our lives. Remember to give people a chance. Mentors come in all shapes and sizes. Those most "like us" may actually offer us the least personal growth. Sometimes I think people come into our lives for a reason or to teach us a lesson, even if they aren't someone that will become a best friend or stay in our life for the next 20 years.

In a disposable society, I sincerely hope we don't start viewing people as disposable too. That isn't what I have been trying to say. Focusing on priorities entails weeding out clutter. This includes trimming, pruning, repairing, and starting seedling relationships.

Clearing physical clutter takes time and effort. Working on our relationships does too. We can't have it all, so don't be afraid to address the people clutter as well as the physical clutter. After all, people are a higher priority than stuff. Right?

CHAPTER 21

VALENTINE'S DAY & LIFE PRIORITIES

Look at the Valentine's Day hype. Am I a better partner if I buy an over-priced card once per year? Does my spouse really prove he loves me if he buys me an expensive piece of jewelry? Will it be a meaningful experience to dine at a crowded restaurant that only gets this over-booked once per year? Is Valentine's Day a retail and restaurant holiday or is it an opportunity to pay attention to important relationships?

It is hard to focus on relationships amid the household clutter and hectic schedules of modern life. It is difficult to drop hectic habits in exchange for simpler ones. Is it possible to make relationships the priority we claim that they are in the midst of an over-scheduled consumerist life style?

People sometimes say they enjoy the simple ideas I teach but they have a hard time implementing them in real life. It is hard to make life changes. Here are techniques to help make lasting changes and to create time to focus on your relationship this Valentine's Day and beyond:

Make one change per week. You know what clutter you want to tackle or life changes you want to make. You don't have the time or energy to do everything at once. It is too daunting. Make one change per week. Small changes add up over time. Reap the cumulative benefit of your efforts to free up your time for your special relationship.

Become a "list person." Put one simple living tip (maybe one you read somewhere—hint, hint) on your weekly to-do list. This gives you a week to accomplish it. That's realistic, right?

Use self-help books to motivate you. A clutter control or time management book is less expensive than hiring a professional organizer or a personal coach. Reread books that have helped in the past. Ideas you weren't ready for on the first read may be do-able now. Plus, a book gives you the flexibility to pick and choose and to tailor ideas to fit your life style.

Stick with new habits for 21 days. Put household clutter in your donation box every day for 21 days. Make Monday and Thursday the new twice-weekly laundry days. Whatever the habit is, establish it by sticking with it for three weeks. Don't forget to reward yourself at the end!

Make contingency plans. People who are most successful at making any kind of life changes are those who create back-up plans right at the beginning. Life has a way of rearing its interfering head right into the middle of your plans. Be ready for it with a fall back plan.

Take care of the basics. You won't get any gold stars. You may not even feel better, yet this basic stuff is some of the best stuff we can do if we value our relationships. I know I've said this before but it bears mentioning again. Take care of physical health checks and dental checkups, as well as life and health insurance. Put wills and death wishes in writing. Set up college financing, and retirement funding. And finally, don't forget to organize all that important paperwork now.

Most of us have at least one thing listed above that we know we could improve, yet we get caught up in daily stuff. We drag our feet. These basics are more important than a clutter-free closet though I can't believe you heard that from me.

A flashy pile of big red roses, a high-calorie expensive meal, or a large box of chocolates (maybe chocolate can be exempt from this example) can be a lot of fun. Initially, this stuff looks appealing. Maybe for the day it carries us. Long term, though, I wonder.

Maybe long term, I'd rather show I care for him and he cares for me through all the little daily stuff. Less clutter and a slower pace are things that ultimately allow us to do better with our relationship. Applying the ideas above to simplify our lives might ultimately have a more lasting effect on our relationship than a flashy piece of jewelry. (Okay, I still fantasize about the flashy jewelry I really don't need.)

CHAPTER 22

VALENTINE'S DAY GIFT: A PROFESSIONAL ORGANIZER

A few years ago, my husband asked me what I would like for Valentine's Day. I told him I did not want food. I was feeling fat. I did not want flowers. They die too quickly. I did not want clothes or jewelry. I was not feeling very flush. I was a writer and a mom, not a fashion queen. I wanted a house call from a professional organizer.

Would you have the courage to let a stranger come into your house to peek into your closets and drawers to critique them? That winter my household clutter and life frustrations overcame my natural desire for privacy. Although it didn't go as planned, it was an inspiring experience.

It would take some courage to let a stranger look inside my closets and drawers, but I hoped it would be worth it. I wanted someone to help me organize my life and my house. I think I wanted to learn how to get better at living my life.

Cabin fever was at my house that winter. The outside walls were creeping closer together. I had no room to put things. There were toys in every room. Piles of stuff kept accumulating on tables, counters and dressers. The laundry was getting harder and harder to squeeze into closets and jam into drawers. The house must have been shrinking.

The kitchen had become a holding tank for all sorts of goodies. Partially completed children's crafts lined the perimeter. School papers lingered on the counter and refrigerator. Tax forms and other paper floated around on the table.

The truth was I needed help. Our household clutter ran more rampant than usual after the holidays. Our home organization needed tweaking. I considered myself to be fairly organized, but I wanted a fresh pair of eyes to check out my situation. Thanks to my husband's Valentine's Day gift of a two-hour visit from a professional organizer, I could do this.

On the appointed day, the professional organizer arrived – 30 minutes late! To her credit, she had called on her way over to tell me she would be late. But I couldn't help wondering if a professional organizer could have been, well, more organized.

When she did get to my house, we quickly rolled up our sleeves and jumped in. Since I had exactly two hours of her time, I wanted to give her an overview of my house for her general suggestions and show her a couple specific problem areas for more detailed advice.

We walked around my house with pen and paper in hand. She noticed the small coat closet at the top of the steps and described the space as "precious." At first I laughed at the term, but then I realized it was accurate. Things in small supply, like diamonds and space in small closets, are precious.

She had some suggestions for how to maximize my small closet. None of them happened to ring my bell. They were good ideas, but I didn't think they would be a fit for my family. That was the first lesson: There are lots of ways to accomplish the same thing. And there is no single perfect solution for each of my clutter concerns.

We went on to the kitchen. She pointed out I really didn't need all the glassware stored in my small kitchen. She was right. I had enough glasses to provide beverages for a party of 60 – more people than I could fit in my house! I got rid of some of it, and I had more room to store things I needed and used more often.

In one of my daughters' bedrooms, she suggested I use one of the closet shelves as a combined storage area and play area for her smaller dolls. I liked that thought but to be honest, I never got around to making the change.

I also asked for her help with the large storage closet in the downstairs den. Everything got tossed there at some point during its life at our house, including books, footwear, dated and off-season clothes, gift-wrapping supplies and holiday decorations.

The organizer provided helpful ideas for grouping these things by function. For example, I had been storing Christmas decorations in several places around the house instead of keeping them together.

She also suggested I journal about or take photos of some of the dated clothing to preserve memories but then promptly donate the clothes themselves. Good idea. I implemented it a few days later.

While the organizer and I were still working, my husband and children appeared exactly two hours after they had left. Unfortunately, I hadn't had a way to let my husband know we started late. It became a little awkward with everyone home, so she left quickly.

After she left, I found her purse on my couch. It didn't seem like a very organized thing for a professional organizer to have done. I left a message on her answering machine so she wouldn't worry. She called me back and stopped by to pick up her purse. When she came back, she said she had enjoyed the quiet time during the drive back to my house. She had children too.

I suppose even the pros have bad days. Even the organized have some disorganization in their lives. I take comfort in the fact that the professional organizer is human, too. I will be easier on myself the next time I am running late and forget my purse. I think it will be OK for me to be less than perfectly organized. Maybe figuring that out was the best Valentine's Day gift of all.

CHAPTER 23

DID YOU GET WHAT YOU WANTED FOR VALENTINE'S DAY?

How did you celebrate Valentine's Day if you happen to have a special romantic person in your life? I love asking people what they did for this not-so-simple holiday. Some people counted themselves lucky if they got a card. Others I talked to got showered with flowers and candy or even a surprise trip to New York! One mom I know looks forward to "BGJ" which is an acronym at her house for "borderline gaudy jewelry."

Valentine's Day in a relationship can feel like walking a tight rope backwards while performing a juggling act. This holiday can exert weird pressure on a relationship. Two totally different sets of expectations may be pitted against each other. She wants a ring and he buys earrings. Or, how does each of us feel if I get him a set of golf clubs and he gets me a box of candy? It can be hard to guess at or create perceived equity or match someone else's expectations even though we all know we are not supposed to keep score and that it is the thought that counts. Yeah, yeah. How can we create a compromise without hurt feelings on one side or resentment on the other?

Valentine's Day can present a communication challenge. How can each person clearly state his or her expectations for the holiday without ruining the romantic surprise? That is, if I have to *tell* him to get me a dozen roses, it doesn't feel quite the same to either of us, does it? On the other hand, is it fair for me to expect him to be psychic and somehow just know what I would like? No.

Earlier I mentioned a unique Valentine's Day gift that I specifically requested from my spouse—a two-hour house call from a professional organizer. Maybe flowers or candy or whatever you exchange is just fine for you. If not, pick a good time to discuss a change of plans for next year with your romantic partner. At least it would allow plenty of time for recovery before next year. Another alternative would be to copy this page for future posting on his bathroom mirror...

I would like to share a few non-traditional Valentine's Day gift ideas that won't add to your closet clutter or your waistline, much. Consider the professional organizer or any other service option for your beloved: upholstery or carpet cleaning, a house cleaner, a painter, or even a window washer. Maybe you could even give the gift of your own time and labor and perform these gifts yourself.

Think about some personal care ideas too. Perhaps your romantic partner would enjoy a retreat—with or without you (especially if there are children in the picture). Maybe he or she would enjoy a professional massage. My spouse gave me a professional massage for my birthday one year. The only down side I saw was that I had to get into my car and drive safely home right after having my entire body turned into melted butter. Another unique gift might be a trip to a day spa for a fun personal care splurge.

Besides the usual dining out (I have to admit I am not a fan of patronizing over-crowded frantic restaurants on this inflated-expectations holiday), consider event options. Ideas include tickets to a concert or a theater performance. Maybe you both could go see a comedy show—*somebody* could be laughing on this day many of us take too seriously!

Another thought is to give the gift of passion. I am talking about giving a unique gift that supports your partner's personal passion. It might mean buying them a class or a seminar related to an interest they have. Maybe you could buy them supplies or equipment for a hobby they enjoy. You could even find them a book or magazine subscription that tracks with their personal passion. Your options here are only limited by how well you know your partner! No pressure.

One year my spouse and I decided to avoid the restaurant scene. We simply exchanged cards and had a nice home date complete with fancy grownup cooking and off-site babysitting. As a weird coincidence, we wound up buying each other identical Valentine's Day cards and even signed them the same way. There was brief confusion when the first person opened their card and thought they'd picked up the wrong one! It wasn't terribly romantic but it was pretty funny.

Another year we simply decided to be practical. We pooled our mythical Valentine's Day budgets and purchased a small item for our home. Exciting? No, but it worked for us. Maybe that is the ultimate point here: Find a Valentine's Day celebration that works for both people in the relationship. Avoid the pitfalls of this funny holiday and figure out a sincere and simple celebration or exchange that works for you and your partner. Don't let the ads fool either of you! Stay focused on your partner and make it a happy Valentine's Day.

~

Section 2

Spring

~

CHAPTER 1

GET CLUTTER HELP FROM SPOUSE & KIDS?

"Getting rid of clutter and organizing my home would be great but I'm not the only one at home, and I can't do it all by myself." This frustration is expressed over and over again by people I talk to about simple living. They don't want to trade in their family (most days). They just want a little more help around the house. To complicate matters, everyone's organizational style and notion of what constitutes adequately "organized" is a little different too.

People are too hard on themselves when they try to "do it all." Nobody can be Superman or Superwoman and take it all on. It is hard to get understanding, support, and help from a busy spouse or children who may not even be aware of the frustrations.

I know I don't have all the answers. If you are willing, I'll share my two cents. These thoughts are based on my own "learning experiences, " what I've picked up from people in my classes, and a few books I'd like to share with you.

First, let's talk about spouses. Sometimes he's the "Oscar" and she's the "Felix" (as in the untidy room-mate and tidy room-mate from *The Odd Couple*). Sometimes it is the other way around. It really doesn't matter who is who. Just the differences in how people living together under the same roof do things can create tensions.

The suggestions below may help you work with a spouse to make positive changes for everyone at home. Some of these ideas may help with children too:

Model it:

Walk Your Talk. Model the behavior changes you are hoping for. This may take years but sometimes it will help (if nothing else, at least it will fix half of the problem). For example, maybe dropping clothing on the bedroom floor is a source of tension. A few years of watching you hop out of bed in the morning without having to step on last night's clothing may make a clear floor begin to look good to your spouse. Your partner may even find a better spot for their clothing than on the floor by the bed.

Explain Your Perspective

Express clutter concerns as your problem, not theirs. Explain how your partner's clutter impairs your ability to perform a function for the family. For example, maybe it is hard to get dinner on the table if it is already full of other things. Saying, "Honey, it is hard for me to set the table for dinner when everyone's stuff is already there" might work better than yelling. (Actually, yelling works too, but then I always need to apologize afterwards for it.)

Ask First

Get permission to touch their stuff and to move it to an agreed upon location. If you have a family member who comes home and dumps their stuff on the kitchen counter or table, it can be frustrating for both of you. You can't use the kitchen space to work on dinner. He can't find his stuff when he wants it because you have moved it. Agree that it is okay for you to move his things to a designated spot, perhaps his desk or dresser top.

Be Specific

Make specific requests when you ask for help. Maybe your partner is willing to help, but doesn't "see" a task like cleaning the kitchen the same way you do. When he helps by cleaning the kitchen, he may diligently wipe behind the bread machine on the counter but leave the fingerprints on the front of the microwave and stove. If you want it done a certain way and he is willing to help, be clear stating specific tasks that will help you the most.

Children's clutter

Now let's talk about children. Simplifying home life with children is another story. Some of them are naturally neat and tidy. Others aren't. Age differences matter too. What works for a three-year-old isn't going to work for a 12-year-old. That said, here are a few general suggestions for all ages.

Include them:

Get children's input when you organize their rooms. If they are involved in the clutter control and organizing process, they will be more likely to use the systems you put in place. If they buy into and use the systems, they will learn helpful life management skills too. And, from a practical standpoint with younger children, they have to be able to physically manage the containers you want them to use. If they can't open and shut the little plastic latch on the box containing their collection of "kid meal" toys, you've just wasted money.

Be extra clear:

Be specific about what household tasks children must do. If they are supposed to clean the bathroom, state that they are expected to clean it by noon on Saturday and that "cleaning the bathroom" includes scrubbing the toilet, wiping the fixtures, mopping the floor...

Teach them as you work with them:

Train children to do the task. This may seem obvious, but don't assume they have magically picked up the necessary skills. Assign age-appropriate tasks. Help them learn how you want things done (after all, it is your house). Show where you want things put away – like where clean dishes from the dishwasher go.

Logical consequences:
Be clear beforehand about consequences if kids don't help. Decide together how many warnings or reminders they will get. Calmly say, "Remember to take out the trash, please." Don't nag or argue. Then, administer the consequence. Dock an allowance or take away a privilege – whatever has been agreed upon. If you are consistent, they will learn.

Patience!
Try to be patient with everyone. I know it is hard enough for me to change my own behavior, much less to get family members to change. Be clear to everyone about the benefits of less chaos which include more time and peace for everyone. If the basic household tasks can be accomplished with less hassle, it is easier on everyone in the family. If one person in the family is happier and more balanced because they are getting some needed help, everyone else will ultimately be happier too.

Some books to help families clear clutter and be organized:
Men are from Mars, Women are from Venus by John Gray may seem like an odd book to suggest for getting help with household chores, but it really isn't. The whole purpose of controlling clutter and getting organized is to free up time and energy for everyone in the home. It is important for spouses to be able to communicate well with each other to accomplish this. If we understand each other's communication styles and approaches, we can work better together. (The techniques in this book really do help! Now, if I could just get my spouse to read the book too...)

How to Organize Your Kid's Room by Susan Isaacs is a small readable book for busy parents. If children are involved in the clutter control and organizing process, they will be more likely to use the systems you put in place. If they buy into and use the systems, they will learn some life management skills too.

Pick Up Your Socks by Elizabeth Crary breaks out help with chores by age. I know when I became a parent I didn't automatically know what household tasks were age appropriate for my kids.

Simplify Your Life with Kids by Elaine St. James with Vera Cole (a mom) has ideas on a variety of kid-related simple living topics. It is full of helpful tips in small concise chapters.

CHAPTER 2

CLEANING TOOLS, PROCRASTINATION, & PERFECTIONISM

The festivities are over. We in cold weather climates settle in for short cold days and long cold nights as we patiently wait for more snow or signs of spring. The walls of my home begin their usual inward march, and it feels like the rooms shrink.

For many, post-holiday finances are tight. Interior home projects loom. Some people are worn out and frustrated by the same old thing while others embrace a return to normal. As for me, I am surprised by the small things I have found to amuse and motivate me.

I received a few new cleaning tools for Christmas. Some of you may groan at this, but I actually asked for them! The "new toys" included microfiber cleaning cloths, a wet mop with built-in cleaning fluid and disposable mop heads, and a lightweight electric hand vacuum with attachments. Now it was time to try them out.

Getting rid of clutter and getting organized excite me. Cleaning doesn't. For me cleaning is tedious and boring. Cleaning doesn't stay done. Have you ever dusted on a bright sunny day and marveled at how the dust swirls up in the air and immediately lands back on the surfaces you've just swiped?

In the past, cleaning has frustrated me and worn me down. But, for now, I am a New Woman. I am transformed! Okay, now I exaggerate, but, really, I am actually excited to clean.

I dart through the house with my new glass-cleaning cloth in hand looking for more dirty surfaces to test it on. I wipe away enthusiastically. I marvel at the lack of lint and chemical residue. I giggle – just a little. I mop. I love not hauling around a sloshy mop bucket of dirty water with chemicals. I thrill at the way the small swivel mop head turns sideways to get behind the bathroom toilet. I rationalize that I'm probably not using any more chemicals than I would dump into a big bucket full of water anyway. I also figure maybe disposable mop heads aren't really frivolously expensive if they motivate me to clean more often. This could save wear and tear on my house... I even use a hand vacuum. I hand vacuum valences, blinds, couch cushions, moldings, and other obscure places. It is fun because I no longer have to drag the heavy tipsy vacuum cleaner along behind me. Because of its short attachment hose, it felt like dragging a large unwilling dog behind me on an extremely short leash. I even read the hand vacuum's instruction manual and played with the assorted attachments. Weird. What is happening to me? Motivation!

If it takes "new toys" to spark a little enthusiasm for cleaning, I'm all for it. Maybe technology has improved tedious chores. Or, maybe trying something new helps me get past my cleaning procrastination and perfectionism.

I procrastinate on household cleaning because it is boring and because of my perfectionism. I have wanted to clean perfectly. That was an unrealistic goal. Now I am in experimental mode. When I am in experimental mode, it is okay to just try something. Besides, if it fails, I can blame the product instead of me.

Finally, what's wrong with having a little fun? Sort of a paradigm shift for home cleaning. Observe. Experiment. Be entertained instead of bored. I suspect the new cleaning toys will reveal their own faults over time, but right now it is just fun, and I'm not worrying about "perfect."

"Perfect" cleaning is a marketing illusion in a magazine advertisement. As Fly Lady at www.flylady.net has said, "Housework done imperfectly still blesses your family." Maybe next time I try to move past my perfectionism, maybe, just maybe, I can try it without the toys.

CHAPTER 3

SPRING CLEANING – TO CLEAN OR NOT TO CLEAN

Spring cleaning is not a favorite activity of mine. In fact, I don't like to clean in spring or any other time. Call me lazy, but I have found the best way to simplify cleaning is to stay clutter-free. Lack of clutter creates the appearance of clean. Lack of clutter makes cleaning easier when I finally do get around to it. I wish I could make cleaning fun. I know some people enjoy it. I usually don't. There are too many other things I would rather spend my time on.

Sadly, at the moment, I can't see clearly out my windows. All the screens are dirty too. My oven needs to be cleaned. The mini blinds that cover most windows in my house have a layer of grime on them thicker than I want to discuss, and you could come over and clearly write your name in the dust on many of my horizontal surfaces —tables, dressers, and the dining room table.

Now that I have laid bare my dirty house to you, so you understand more of my shortcomings, let me share the things I have learned. My formula for simple spring cleaning success consists of four ingredients – motivation, proper cleaning products, professional cleaning techniques, and a helpful home. I hope these are helpful cleaning tips for any season. When these ingredients are there, the rest is simple.

Motivation.
For me having company over once in a while is a good thing. It forces me to tackle cleaning projects I have been putting off. It sounds weird, but sometimes I even pretend company is coming

over or I pretend I am having an open house. The benefit of getting these postponed jobs done is how great I feel afterwards. The sad thought is, why do I need company to clean? Couldn't I be happy to clean for us? For my family and myself? That ought to be sufficient motivation right there.

Proper cleaning products.

First, check out products around the house that you've been hanging onto. Maybe there are a few products you tried but didn't work for you, or they just didn't become part of your cleaning routine. Even though you "paid good money for them," you are not using them. Rather than letting them continue to age and fill up storage space in your home, toss them by taking them to a recycling center if possible. Instead of feeling bad every time you see unused products sitting there under your sink, feel bad once as you properly and safely dispose of them.

Most cleaning experts agree you only need a few basics for household cleaning – a glass cleaner, a general cleaner, and an anti-bacterial cleaner. The other thing they suggest is owning decent microfiber cleaning cloths that are large enough to fold and use. Have quality dusters that grab the dust instead of just push it around. Look into electrostatic cloths or wool dusters. Decent cleaning rags won't leave their own lint behind while you clean – come on, I suspect that is one reason why some don't like to clean. Right?

It is also time to make friends with your vacuum cleaner. Pull the threads off the beater bar regularly and change the bag frequently (before it is overflowing). Know how to replace the belts. Should you dust or vacuum first? See Don Aslett's book *Do I Dust Or Vacuum First?: Answers to the 100 Toughest, Most Frequently Asked Questions about Housecleaning.* Don Aslett is my favorite house cleaning and clutter author. Gravity works. Dust first, knocking the dirt to the floor and then vacuum it up. If you have an air filter on your furnace, run your furnace fan while you vacuum to catch the dust that vacuuming may stir up.

Professional cleaning techniques.

Why not clean like the pros do? Check out Don Aslett's book *Is There Life After Housework?* or Jeff Campbell's book *Speed Cleaning*. These authors started their careers by being professional cleaners. Each author started and ran a commercial cleaning business. They know their stuff.

Helpful home.

Consider working toward a self-cleaning house (you can read about Don Aslett's in one of his books). Anyone can work toward this. A self-cleaning house begins with Don Aslett's basic rule: "Shoes off at the door. No exceptions." Experts agree that 90 per cent or more of the dirt in our homes comes right in the door. If you stop it at the door, you have won more than half the battle.

Another part of a self-cleaning house is commercial grade indoor and outdoor entry mats. If not a commercial grade indoor mat, at least make sure it is washable when it becomes saturated with dirt and grime.

A self-cleaning house also has low or easy maintenance flooring and window treatments. Consider low height, neutral, dirt-hiding, carpet. If the fibers are short, wear and crushing are less evident. Carpet that has flecking, like a cut Berber, hides dirt too. Nylon carpet wears longer than some of the others. Also, fibers with a tight twist won't loosen as quickly or pill as fast. When comparing carpeting, look at the number of twists per inch.

Window treatments that don't cover up too much of the window and block light are a favorite of mine. I like no valences or short valences that are easy to dust and easy to slide off and throw in the washing machine. I combine valences with pleated shades or mini blinds. A friend taught me that the easy way to wash blinds is simply to wash them in the bathtub.

A final element of a helping home is the furnishings – sturdy fabrics, neutral dirt-hiding colors, and patterns and designs that hide minor stains or spots. When I put a solid hunter green tablecloth on my dining room table, every speck of lint, dust, and dog hair in my house seems to land on it. When I put a lighter multicolored floral tablecloth there, it usually looks clean for weeks.

I am going to conclude by using the "h" word" – "habits." Cleaning is easier if I regularly pick up (get rid of clutter) and perform minimal weekly cleaning. I vacuum my carpet without moving furniture, dust lightly, and swipe sinks and toilets every few days. I also try to make it a habit to quickly straighten a room every time I leave it.

When I keep to a schedule (think of this as a less frequent habit) for some of the tougher jobs, I am happier. Tasks may not get done as often as they "should" be, but at least they are getting done. Frankly, I have found less frequent cleaning won't hurt most things – less frequently changing bedding or towels, or deep cleaning the bathroom, or edging with the vacuum cleaner... No one has noticed a difference, and I have freed up some of my time.

Well, that is it for my simple spring cleaning. I hope simplifying and reducing cleaning tasks frees up time for you to enjoy spring. Consider this – if there is dust on the coffee table, but everyone is outside playing, who needs to worry about it?

CHAPTER 4

KNOW THIS *BEFORE* YOU SPRING CLEAN: DONATION VALUES

Who doesn't like a win-win situation? Spring clean your clutter away and earn money in the process. Some people enjoy weeding out clutter and holding spring garage sales. For other people, it is simpler to donate clutter than to have a garage sale.

For non-cash tax-deductible donations, you can make itemized lists including descriptions and values of what you donate. Sometimes, though, it can be difficult to determine a fair "garage sale value" to put down for each item. Or, if you do plan to have a garage sale, it can be equally difficult to figure out how to price items for your sale.

How do you know what that floral print dress is worth? How much could you put down for the black leather shoes? The decision-making process of trying to determine the right dollar values to write down can make the whole clutter control and donation/garage sale process more difficult. For taxes, we have been told to put down "garage sale" values, but that still might leave you wondering if you are "doing it right." Who wants to get into trouble with the IRS?

Look at the website at http://turbotax.intuit.com/personal-taxes/itsdeductible/index.jsp. It looks like Turbo Tax partnered with ItsDeductible.The ItsDeductible software simplifies valuing your donated items by providing values for thousands of commonly donated items. The company is called Income Dynamics, Inc., and it also sells a book called *Its Deductible, 2002 - Cash for Your Used Clothing and Thousands of Commonly Donated Items*.

If you would like to work with a professional organizer to

clear out and itemize your clutter, try: www.organizerswe bring.com or www.napo.net. You can search for one by state to find one in your area.

Will your professional organizer come back to support you if you get audited? Probably not, so play it safe. Talk to a tax professional. Write down everything you donate, including item description and value, and attach photos and/or receipts if you have them. "Doing it right" could earn you money or save you money as you send your accumulated clutter out into the world to those who could have a genuine need for those things.

Organize your garage sale/donation items simply. Line a large cardboard box with a trash bag. Keep a legal pad and pen clipped to your donation box so that you can quickly jot donations down as you toss them in. Itemizing as you go may be easier than accumulating a bag or box of stuff that you have to go through again later. Choose the method that works best for you.

It may be too late to do anything for this year's taxes. But, as you gear up for a little spring-cleaning and get ready to clear out clutter before summer, these resources may help you to prepare for this year's garage sale or next year's tax season.

CHAPTER 5

ONE PERSON'S TRASH IS ANOTHER PERSON'S TREASURE: RESPONSIBLE DONATING

I am a thrift store and garage sale shopper, so I whole-heartedly agree with the old adage "One person's trash is another person's treasure."

This is also true when we weed out our homes to free ourselves of clutter. When I speak about clutter control, I encourage people to find homes for their items where they will be more appreciated than they are now. I also find it easier to get rid of clutter in my home and part with my precious "treasures" if I feel they will wind up where they will be needed and appreciated. It is easier for me to live without fourteen "extra" pairs of blue jeans if I know they are going to help people who may not have any blue jeans at all.

People who attend my classes and seminars often feel the same way. They want to free up time and energy for themselves by parting with their extraneous clutter, but they want to free themselves from clutter conscientiously.

Here are some ideas to help "spring clean" responsibly.

Charity begins at home.
Donate locally if possible. A local church store, shelter, or food shelf may be more than happy to accept your items. I am a fan of supporting and taking care of your local community.

Donate items that are clean and in decent condition.
Many organizations that accept donations do not do any repairs or cleaning. Please donate items that still have some life in them

and are in reasonable shape. Make decisions about what to donate with humanity so recipients of your donations can receive them with dignity.

Carefully wrap and pack any breakables so they aren't destroyed in transit.

This sounds like common sense, but sometimes we get in a hurry when we are getting rid of clutter. Don't let donation items turn into broken trash just from poor packing.

Call the charity if in doubt about something you are donating.

See if they will take the item. If they won't, they may be able to suggest who might accept it. Be aware that charities update their lists frequently. What an organization accepts can change quickly over time, so call or check their website first. If they receive items they can't use, they may have to put them in the trash.

Donate to an organization that supports a cause that matters to you.

Check out United Way's "Community Resource Directory" which many libraries have, or look up their website for information on a variety of charitable organizations in your area. This site explains the services organizations provide in the community and sometimes it lists what kinds of donations they can accept.

Consider charitable organizations that make house calls to get donations.

Save yourself the time to deliver your donations by having them picked up at your home.

There are many options out there for gently used "extra" goods. Please consider responsible donating next time you are in a clutter control mood, or try some of these thoughts now if you are ready to do a little spring cleaning.

CHAPTER 6

CANDY, CANDY, CANDY: CHILDREN'S EASTER CLUTTER

Candy, candy, candy! It happens every year in April, but it doesn't stop there. Sometimes a few not-so-fresh candy Easter eggs wait to be discovered behind sofa legs and in odd corners when I deep clean my house in November for the holidays. Yummy. As a "sometimes organized" mom, I have been known to snare the Easter Bunny before he leaves my house for a tally of the hidden treats to prevent such "delicious" finds later in the year. I confess: I do this because I would be too embarrassed to have to explain to the dentist why I tried to break a tooth on a six-month old jellybean. Easter Bunny and I have worked for years to simplify my children's Easter candy feast. As well-meaning parents in the early years, my spouse and I tried to save our children's teeth by sacrificing our own waistlines. Full of good intentions after Easter, we stood at the kitchen counter after the children were in bed and selflessly and unabashedly grazed on Easter baskets crammed full of candy.

After barely putting a dent in this dangerous display of bounty, we'd get picky. We disposed of the off-brand candy and then kept and selflessly ate the good stuff with our children. Over the years, we figured there had to be a better, less wasteful, and more ethical way to curtail the candy.

There are as many candy traditions, as there are homes that celebrate Easter. There's no single way to go about it, but here are a few solutions that may help simplify the Easter candy feast.

Smaller quantities. If you aren't too deeply entrenched in overly bountiful traditions yet, set more reasonable, realistic expectations about candy quantities. Sometimes E.B. limits the quantity to what fits in one small basket and then hides the basket. In other homes, E.B. hides the individual eggs to prolong the pleasure of the hunt yet he still holds the quantity down.

Provide variety by splitting bags of candy with another family or two. Do you like the speckled malted milk chocolate eggs, the cream filled eggs, the candy bar flavored eggs, or the marsh-mallow peeps? Sharing is a fun way to discover other families' candy traditions, and no one winds up with large quantities just for the sake of having a wide variety. Just because Easter candy is packaged 24 to a box doesn't mean you can't exchange and share it before the hunt.

Encourage well-meaning grandparents, aunts, and uncles to look at the big candy picture, all candy your children will receive from all sources. Perhaps E.B. would be willing to leave smaller quantities for your children at relatives' homes in consideration of everything your children receive cumulatively that day. Try suggesting non-candy options too.

Anyone can ask the E.B. to substitute small gifts or trinkets for candy. Money, stickers, small dime store variety toys, key chains, children's jewelry, and fast food or movie gift certificates fit easily inside plastic eggs. Or small presents, like egg-shaped sidewalk chalk, can be wrapped in spring-time wrapping paper. E.B. sometimes uses a different wrapping paper pattern for each child and puts a small sample of their paper in their Easter basket so they know what to hunt for.

If your children still end up with too much candy, use it up quickly. A quick binge for a few days may be easier on the teeth than a protracted sugar bath that lasts for weeks. Donate any extra unopened candy to a food shelf or take some in to work for a few days to share with co-workers.

Finally, save a bunny and save some money. For young children, consider trading stuffed toy bunnies with another family. A quick count of my children's stuffed animals reveals a disproportionate quantity of bunnies compared to other animal species. It makes sense. Every Easter, well-meaning family members add to my children's bunny collections. My children have more bunnies than they know they have. They haven't even played with many of them. Instead of purchasing more, consider swapping some of these like-new bunnies with another family.

Reduce quantities of candy and stuff gradually from year to year if you need to. Create family spiritual activities, Easter meal menus, and family egg coloring traditions to interest the children from year to year. Take some of the focus away from the candy. Keep your own family Easter traditions by making a few notes from year to year and keeping them in an Easter folder. After all, E.B. still wouldn't want to forget the dark chocolate maple cream Easter eggs when he stops at our house!

CHAPTER 7

BODY CLUTTER: THE "D" WORD—DIET!

I joined Weight Watchers. With breakfast, a heavy sweater, and me, I weighed in at 40 pounds above the average weight I had maintained for most of my adult life. Where did this body clutter come from? (Besides Easter, I mean.) I used to think purchasing disposable items didn't count toward increasing household clutter. After all, paper towels, toilet paper, and food get used up. If I tote these items home and enjoy them with family and friends, none of it lingers on to become clutter. That was my theory. I was wrong.

Some of the food has lingered on, on me. Sigh. It happened gradually. It honestly was fun. I enjoyed the food. However, it couldn't go on. It just wasn't healthy, and I wanted to have more energy for my priorities. Who would have guessed that clutter control would include diet? Argh, it is the ugly "D" word.

Recent attempts to lose weight included the trendy deprivation crash diets. They didn't work for me like they had when I'd gained a mere five to ten pounds. Maybe I'm too far gone, or my metabolism has finally changed. Maybe I'm no longer into torturing myself with a trendy diet, or maybe I just can't stick with the self-abuse long enough to drop the kind of weight I'm talking about.

What I need is a long-term life change in my eating habits, not a quick fix. This realization brought me to Weight Watchers. Slow and steady will win the race. Did you know the rabbit gave up on the third day and binged on cheese and chocolate while the tortoise won the race?

Maybe two pounds per week doesn't seem fast enough. I look at it this way: Time marches on regardless of what I do or don't do. The next twenty weeks will happen with or without me on a more reasonable eating plan. Results don't need to come fast. They just need to come.

How did I get here in the first place? Good times. They were everywhere. You don't realize, until you try to diet, how much a person's social life revolves around eating – dinner out, get-togethers with food, and even meeting for "coffee." I repeatedly made poor but tasty choices in social situations.

What else? Stress. When my kids fight with each other or with me, chances are you will find me at the refrigerator door – as though stuffing something in my face will stuff my frustrations. And, if there is a stressful task I don't want to do, I can stall by grabbing a snack, and later, I can have another treat to reward myself when I am done.

Next is plain old boredom. What's a gal to do to kill time? It feels satisfying to munch on something. In fact, it has been so pleasurable, that I've indulged too often. I've learned to perform boring mundane tasks while snacking, and snacking, and snacking.

Finally, it TASTES GOOD! Let the flavors live on! I don't want it to end. No. Now I have to pay the piper. I enjoy flavors. Why do the best flavors seem to have the most calories, fat, and/or carbohydrates? It just isn't fair, but that's the way it is. I do like the flavor of broccoli and brussel sprouts, but I'll never rank them above chocolate and red wine.

Why do I wish to slim down? It is time to get rid of the body clutter that is weighing me down physically and emotionally. Clutter really does take many forms.

If you think weight loss plans just teach common sense, you may be right. But, obviously, some of us could use a reminder. I realized I was in trouble at my first meeting when the leader asked what people liked to have for breakfast. I figured a can of diet pop wasn't the right answer, so I kept my hand down. In spite of common sense, bad habits have crept into my life.

Weight Watchers or any other plan isn't easy, but I figure payment and weekly weigh-ins keep me accountable. After all, I want to get my money's worth, and now I'm not just answering to myself. It is going to take time. Like peeling back the physical clutter in closets and drawers, it is going to come off in layers, a little at a time just like it crept into my life.

Portion sizes are key. Half an old-me portion size doesn't mean half the satisfaction. It may mean about 85 per cent of the satisfaction for half the calories and fat. Portion sizes. If I don't un-supersize my portions, then I will not be able to un-supersize myself! Less is more!

Slow and steady will win any race. Unlike deprivation diets, I can eat anything I want with Weight Watchers if I've budgeted my points for it. That means that if I have a craving, I can address it—I may not be able to fully satisfy it, but at least I can try. This makes more sense to me than a deprivation diet that has me fantasizing about a single saltine cracker by the third day.

CHAPTER 8

CLUTTER CLEARING HOME DECORATING IDEAS

The trick to simple home decorating, if there is one, is to have a home that reflects and enhances your life. Unfortunately, other things, like clutter, often creep in. Visual clutter can weigh us down.

One couple I know has a nearly full wine rack above the refrigerator in their kitchen. From a simple decorating standpoint, I have a problem with this. Why? Because I happen to know neither of them likes to drink wine! Hey, check out the dust collector!

Another family has a large, beautiful, and very expensive stand mixer on their kitchen counter. Why do I shake my head? Because I know they don't bake, except maybe a little at Christmas.

A woman I know has several beautiful, though dusty, candles on a living room table. What bewilders me? I know she won't ever light them because she is afraid of causing a fire. That is an understandable concern, so why bother with the candles?

What do all three of these situations have in common? They are unauthentic decorating choices that clutter instead of beautify their homes. In my opinion, decorating would do more for people if it enhances their home life. To achieve this, consider decorating items that are authentic, functional, and simple for you.

Authentic decorating

Your home is your castle. It is not "The Jones"'castle. Since this is where you nest, entertain, and generally hang out (at least on weekends), let your home express your personal hobbies, interests, and color preferences.

If you don't like to drink wine, why keep a wine rack with dusty bottles in your kitchen? People who really like wine store most of it in a cool, dark place, like a wine cellar or basement.

It is okay to decorate to reflect the potential for fun at home, just like the magazines do, but make sure it is your idea of fun. Choose art and colors that make you happy instead of matching the current trend. This means the art might be a reflection of your family's travels, hobbies, or interests. This approach is authentic, frugal and more enduring – your preferences probably don't change as often as the cover of a home decorating magazine.

Buy art and other decorations you like instead of worrying about whether or not they match your window coverings. Remove dusty faded valences and drapes. Make a conscious decision about whether or not you want your window décor and privacy options to block part of the window. Consider blinds or pleated shades if you don't want to cover up the window. Take note of what you like and keep a clipping file for your emerging personal decorating style.

Functional Decorating

Functional decorating means filling your precious dwelling space with things that work for you, not against you. Why move, clean, and wipe under a heavy stand mixer on the counter if you don't regularly use it? Put kitchen tools you enjoy using frequently on your counter and store the rest elsewhere. Better yet, don't own that other stuff.

How about combining decorating and functionality? Use decorative baskets or boxes in colors and styles that excite you to store your magazines and hobbies where you can easily reach them. Put decorative mirrors in places you need them, and use them to maximize space and light in small dark places.

Don't over-decorate in rooms that need regular thorough

cleaning, like the kitchen or bathroom. Dried silk flowers and knick-knacks that get dusty and dripped on don't belong in these spaces.

Remember the universal law of dirt: light items show dark dirt. Dark items show light dirt. And, most household dirt is light. At our house, we chose light-haired dogs (yellow instead of black lab) to go with our already light-colored carpet.

Simple Decorating

My favorite approach. People know their authentic personal preferences. They also know what items in their lives are functional. They wonder how to decorate to simplify their lives, or at least their spring cleaning! Here are a few simple decorating tips. When in doubt, go back to the first two thoughts – authentic and functional.

Decorate "Big." Use a few large pieces instead of a lot of little things that must be moved around all the time to clean and dust. Use one large figurine or bowl to catch the eye instead of many little items on a table competing for attention.

Decorate vertically instead of horizontally. That is, try to put interesting items up on the walls instead of cluttering table and counter surfaces. Try large wall hangings and bright big tablecloths to make a change or reflect the seasons of the year. Remember, if you miss the dusty candles or little stuff, you can set them back out again. This isn't rocket science! It is just home decorating.

Natural colors often look better than artificial colors. There is no substitute for using real fruit and flowers to add color to a home. Fill a pretty bowl in the kitchen with fruit – just make sure it is fruit your family likes to eat!

Buy a couple of potted flowers like azaleas or get a bucket filled with an assortment of bulbs that bloom at different times for the living room or family room. They will last for weeks and are a better value for your dollar than cut flowers. They can brighten your home and your attitude especially if you are in a hurry for spring.

Enhance your home with scents you like – baking bread, baking cookies (invite me over, please), or any other cooking. Try scented candles, or a simple pot pourri on the stovetop – a pan of water with some cut up fruit such as oranges and apples tossed in with spices like cinnamon and nutmeg. Be careful. Don't let it burn dry and wreck a pan or become a fire hazard!

Show off your family and encourage discussion. Display family and vacation photos in attractive-to-you picture frames. If you are a parent, grandparent, or other recipient of "kid art," show it off in "real" picture frames. This will thrill the young artist, beautify your home, and make a great conversation piece. If, like me, you hate to move a lot of frames to dust tables, hang them on the walls instead.

Change a few simple things every few weeks to keep your interest. It isn't necessary to go out and buy new stuff all the time. Sometimes shifting around what you already have will sufficiently perk up a room.

Finally, find a balance between "warmth and character" and "chaos and clutter" that works for you and your family. Most importantly, enjoy! This is *your* castle!

Easy activities to simplify home decorating

1. Browse through your favorite catalog at your leisure without dragging your family to the mall.
2. Jot down and tear out ideas you like when you see them in a catalog or magazine.
3. Look at each room of your home. Create a decorating "wish list" for each room. Stick with the list and don't create clutter by adding extras.
4. Remove clutter and create some empty spaces in your home. Wait to see what you really want to put in these spaces. Maybe you will discover the joy of having more

open space!

5. Clean, repair, and appreciate what you already have. Be grateful for what you already have!

Lauri Ward, author of *Use What You Have Decorating* and *Trade Secrets from Use What You Have Decorating* offers simple decorating solutions that use the stuff we already have! She has a website at www.redecorate.com Her many "before" and "after" pictures and her very specific and detailed ideas are very helpful.

CHAPTER 9

POTHOLES & PRIORITIES—KEEP AN EYE ON THE BIG PICTURE

Have you ever observed or participated in spring's pothole avoidance driving? Sudden swerves left or right, or up onto curbs, or briefly over centerlines? We aren't dozing behind the wheel; we're simply dodging potholes – from widening cracks to big car-swallowing caverns that lead directly to the center of the Earth. I can't help wondering how many accidents happen as a result of attempts to avoid potholes. Do we remember to keep an eye out for the big picture?

Several years ago, a woman came to one of my simple living classes. As the evening progressed, her comments and insights told me she was already very clutter-free and well organized. I wondered why she had taken the class. Toward the end of the night, she asked me what to do about newspaper clutter. "Aha," I thought to myself as I envisioned mounds of old newspapers stacked on tables and piled on the floor next to chairs in her home.

I asked her to describe the newspaper clutter. She said she didn't like seeing today's, and maybe yesterday's newspaper floating around on her kitchen table or counter. She felt it looked messy. That was it. A small clutter concern. I suggested a magnetic basket on the side of her refrigerator or a flat-sided hanging basket for her kitchen wall. Either of these options would get the newspapers off her horizontal kitchen surfaces yet still keep them available to read in the kitchen.

Years later I realized my mistake. All I did was show her how to avoid a very small pothole. I had been given the opportunity to help her and other students in the class avoid major accidents, and all I taught them was how to swerve a little. I could have asked her if she had taken care of her "big picture" items as well as she had addressed her clutter concerns. I define "big picture" items as people's true priorities as well as plans for the basic facts of life.

Several years ago, one of my brothers-in-law died suddenly and unexpectedly of a heart attack at the age of 49. Without warning, he left behind his wife, daughter, parents, and brothers. As I, and anyone else who has gone through an experience like this can tell you, when something like this happens, you find out in a hurry what your priorities are and what really matters.

The week of his death was completely different than the week any of us had previously written out on our calendars. The daily "busy-ness" of our lives just didn't matter. Supporting each other and getting through each day the best we could became our priorities. In the midst of our shock and grief, we were thrown into planning a visitation, a funeral, and a burial for a dear family member. I watched my sister-in-law agonize over important choices that hadn't been discussed with her husband during life, including organ donation, and funeral, and burial wishes.

As time moved on, my husband and I realized there were many priorities we needed to address ourselves in the coming weeks and months. The pile of newspapers on the kitchen table can be distracting clutter that keeps us from our priorities, but there are some basics that have a higher priority than clutter control.

Health: Without health, very little can be undertaken or enjoyed. Make sure everyone in the family is current in their physical checkups and their dental checkups. Schedule appointments now if needed. Carry adequate health insurance and know where you could quickly locate your benefits binder when you need it.

Death: Death isn't an "if." It is a "when." Taking care of the family is a priority for many of us in life. Take care of them in death too. No one knowingly chooses to leave his or her family with a mess. Have a current will, adequate life insurance, and detailed death, funeral, and burial/ cremation wishes spelled out now. Consider organ donation too.

Life: Life will go on. Once you have the above items in place, can someone step in and manage your household? Do they know where you stash your bills, file your records, have your financial assets and debts, and keep your life insurance paperwork and other important documents? Could they find the location of your safety deposit box? You don't have to give up your privacy now, but consider creating a folder with this information. Tell the person who would settle your affairs where they can find this folder.

All of us will experience a death in the family. Eventually we find it easy and comfortable to slip back into our normal, routine "busy-ness." We are all human. Sometimes it is easier to work on the little stuff than the big stuff. Recognizing this, I still try to encourage people to take care of their big stuff first. It will be time well spent. It doesn't make sense to spend all of our time dodging the little potholes of life if we haven't taken care of our major priorities.

CHAPTER 10

CLUTTER AGAIN – PEELING BACK THE LAYERS

Clutter. Clutter. Clutter. Clutter seems to be the home issue that people who attend my seminars struggle with the most. I struggle with it too, to the point where wrestling the clutter demon and helping others wrestle with it has become my passion.

Maybe clutter is simply a natural part of the human condition? I hope not! The pervasive feelings about clutter seem to be angst and guilt. We struggle with our clutter and we feel bad about our struggle. What is the answer? Maybe we could just give up some of the angst. Recognize that clutter sometimes must come off in layers. It would be nice if it could all come off in a weekend in one giant purge, but because of human nature and real life, it just doesn't work that way.

My college textbooks and paperwork are a perfect example of why clutter sometimes has to come off in layers. Since I had invested a lot of time and energy in studying, I initially felt the books and notes somehow represented who I was. I couldn't purge this clutter at all years ago. It would have felt like throwing away my education! After a few years, I was able to toss the notes and textbooks for subjects that weren't critical to my majors. Later, I realized that I wouldn't really go back to all the notes I'd taken, even in my professional field, so I recycled that box of paper too. More recently, I realized the textbooks had become dated and it was time to let go of them too. All that remains are a few papers I wrote that I keep because I get a kick out of them, and I hang onto the illusion that my kids might get a kick out of them some day – as though they're going to have time to read Mom's old papers (yeah, right).

I could beat myself up over the fact it took me years to get rid of my college clutter, or I can accept it and get on with it. I learned that I simply needed to make it a habit to regularly address clutter, just like teeth brushing or laundry. I decided to drop the angst and guilt over the fact that I often can't toss my clutter all at once. You can too.

Here are clutter fighting techniques:

- Make it a habit to regularly "sweep" through a room, or even just a drawer, to cull items that haven't been used in a reasonable period of time. Keep in mind that our sense of time has a way of getting distorted. If I think I haven't used that salad mold for a year or so, but that I might still use it again "some day," chances are I really haven't used it in over two years and I won't use it in the future either.

- Pretend to move across the country. As I look at each item in a room, I ask myself if I would be willing to pack it up and move it across the country (this is my fantasy move to the location of my dreams). If I would not take it there, why would I let this item hang around here in my present day home?

- Ask yourself what your grown children will do with an item you are reluctant to toss when they find it in the bottom of the closet some day. Will they know what it is? Will they know the family history behind this treasure? Will they recognize its value*? If they will see no value in it, why hang onto it? *If it has value, make sure your kids know the value (sentimental or financial) now.

- Recognize evolution. Styles, colors, and technology constantly change for almost everything. Think about stereo equipment, records, video cassettes, vacuum cleaners, microwavable dishes, and baby clothes. Ask yourself if the item you are clinging to will stand the test of time. If not, send it on its way now.

It is okay for clutter to come off in layers, especially if I am willing to make it a habit to address my clutter regularly. Life constantly changes. People constantly change. Our definition of clutter today isn't the same as how we will define it tomorrow. Maybe clutter is kind of like an onion. We get to peel it off in layers!

CHAPTER 11

COMMON SENSE CLUTTER CONTROL

There are too many places in my house (and basement, and car, and garage...) to store too much stuff. I have this nagging feeling that if I could get rid of half of my stuff my life would be simpler. I even suspect I wouldn't miss anything. I dare to think I'd have more time and energy if I didn't spend so much time cleaning, tidying, sorting, and weeding out household stuff.

The problem is that when I look at the stuff I have tucked away, it all seems like "good stuff." Much of it is useful and in good condition. So what's the issue? Sheer quantity!

Why can't I get rid of it? I have a poor memory. Yes, poor memory creates clutter. When I'm weeding out the basement closet, I forget what I have in the hallway and bedroom closets. It doesn't all fit in my head at once. This makes for incomplete clutter control.

There is a simple solution — a common sense clutter control rule to help:

Group like things together. It sounds like a science experiment, but it is actually an organizing rule that helps get rid of household clutter and keeps it from coming back. Although I had read it before in clutter control and organizing books, I couldn't see why it mattered or how it applied to me. Finally, one day, I got it.

I was looking for a picture frame. I had a cute kid photo I wanted to display. I checked the kitchen drawer and looked at the frames there. Next, I went to my bedroom and pulled out other photo frames tucked away in a dresser. After that, I went downstairs and looked through the desk, and finally, I dug through some frames I had tucked away in the laundry room. Are you fed up yet? I was. I was running around my house like a hamster in a cage checking out food stashes.

Oh… "Group like things together." I finally got it. I gathered all my picture frames together. I tossed the broken ones. I donated the ones that I didn't like or were funny sizes or that didn't match my decorating ideas. At last, I was left with a small stack of frames that I put in a box on a shelf in the laundry room.

The trick is to apply this rule to all clutter categories of life. I can't weed out clothing until I'm caught up with the laundry and have all the clothing together. I can't effectively weed out shoes until I'm looking at every pair I own. That means I have to grab the pairs in the bedroom, the ones in the entry closet, and the ones downstairs and put them all together.

What about my husband's sports jackets and baseball caps? We have to grab the ones in the bedroom closet, the ones in the spare closet, the ones on his workbench, and the ones out in his truck to get an accurate count of what he really has.

What about my children's books, games, or toys? If some of their stuff is in their bedrooms and some of it is tucked in the toy room, family room, basement, or garage, then they will have the same problem with weeding out.

At our house, we gather together things like videos, CD's, stuffed animals, and mittens. Group like things together in each clutter category to make lasting decisions about what to donate, what to save, and what storage containers will keep us better organized.

Store like items together. This is an important corollary to the first rule. Once you have gathered up like items, try to designate one place to store them together. No one really wants to spend time hunting all around the house looking in several places for one kind of thing.

When someone looks for something at your house, do you

ever find yourself telling them, "Well, check here, or, if it's not here, try over there, or maybe it will be in such and such a spot, and have you looked in the (fill in the blank) yet?" When possible, any single category of stuff would be easier to find and manage if it has only one storage spot in the home.

I don't want to purchase extra stuff just because I can't find the one I already own. Most importantly, I don't want to waste time weeding out clutter over and over again because I can only make partial decisions. I can't keep a complete inventory in my head as I move from closet to closet and room to room.

Finally, think like a PRO. That is, to **P**ile like items together, **R**educe the quantity, and then **O**rganize the remainder. Try the simple rules and acronym to weed out household clutter once — and for all.

CHAPTER 12

GARAGE SALE SHOPPING – ONE MOM'S IDEA OF FASHION, FUN & FRUGALITY

Once upon a time we moved to White Bear Lake, Minnesota and bought our first home. I panicked. How was I going to fill all those empty rooms when we moved from our small rental? At that moment a garage "sailor" was born. I continue to learn the tricks and traps of the trade, and garage sale and newspaper ad decor still grace our home.

Our used Ethan Allen dining room set had matching maple corner hutches purchased at different sales several years apart. I also purchased tables, couches, and two bedroom sets. Smaller purchases included an oak corner hutch for the kitchen, a spring horse for the children, and an oak glider rocker.

My friends sometimes call me the "garage sale queen." (I am not sure it is always a compliment even though they seem impressed with the bargains.) Before you knock it, try it. Garage sale, newspaper, and Internet shopping has increased in popularity. It is fashionable, environmentally sound, frugal and fun.

More people are beginning to appreciate the benefits of reusing and recycling goods. Shopping at garage sales can be inexpensive, entertaining, and social. It's a great way to satisfy that "shopper's itch" without getting into a lot of trouble. Twenty dollars can go a long way in shopping power and entertainment value for an afternoon. Since I "hunt" a lot in my hometown, I frequently run into people I know, which adds to the fun.

Unusual and interesting finds make it an adventure. I once bought a very used wok for two dollars just for its plastic footed base. Our own broken wok base made our wok tip when we cooked. I felt very self-sufficient when I proudly screwed in the "new" base.

Children and adults can enjoy trendy things without paying top prices. I found a remote-controlled toy school bus for $5. Similar toys retail for $35. I found a new terracotta garlic roaster for $2. I used it several times before deciding it used too much storage space in my small kitchen – a less costly mistake than buying it new would have been.

Garage sale season in Minnesota is relatively short. Depending on the weather, it runs from April through September. Sales usually start toward the end of the week and run into the weekend. Many even offer evening hours for those who have day jobs.

Find garage sales advertised in the newspaper and posted on signs in the neighborhoods. Check the newspaper a day or two before you plan to go for locations and times or enjoy an unplanned stop when you spot a sign. Check out my hunting strategies below.

My favorite "hunting" strategies:

Have a shopping list. Include items for you as well as things you know friends and family members want. Write down sizes.

Study the ads. Many include the size and gender of children's clothing. They may also list big-ticket items and indicate if they have any tools, furniture, and household items.

Serious garage sale shoppers plan a route based on locations and starting times for sales. Identify sales that interest you. Group them together by geographic location and starting times. Use a map book to plan your route to avoid backtracking, wasting time, and getting lost. Try to get to the best sales a few minutes before they open.

Shop with an open mind for sport and fun. Enjoy browsing for the fun of it and be prepared to come across the unusual or unexpected.

Carry enough cash. This might be 20 to 50 dollars – more if you are shopping for big-ticket items like furniture. Many people let you put down a deposit to hold a big-ticket item. Sometimes you can write a check to hold it and then trade your check for your cash when you come back to get your purchase.

Sometimes you find the best goods on the first day of a sale. You may find the best bargains on subsequent days as sellers become more willing to reduce prices and negotiate. My friend Carla suggests looking for second or third day bag sales where you can fill up a grocery bag with whatever you want for a couple of dollars.

Be philosophical, not mean-spirited. If you miss the perfect widget someone is walking away with just as you arrive or if someone snags a super bargain from a table right under your nose, it just wasn't meant to be that day. Consider it a learning experience.

When you get to a sale, scan it quickly for obvious deals. Next, thoroughly review what's there so you don't miss any goodies hidden in the visual clutter.

Prices at garage sales can vary widely. After you have a few sales under your belt, you get a feel for the prices for common items. Now you can recognize great deals when you find them.

Helpful buying strategies:

Say "hi," make eye contact, and be pleasant to break the ice and ease the discomfort of being in someone else's garage. Friendliness on the front end makes it more comfortable and may improve your negotiating success in a few minutes.

Negotiate. Negotiate. Negotiate. All I mean is don't be afraid to ask! "I really like this widget. Would you be willing to take five dollars for it?" The worst they will say is no. They may make a counter offer. When you find several items you want, you can total up their prices and offer a reduced figure for the entire lot.

Be prepared to walk away, or feel free to change your mind and pay full price.

Remember there is no return policy. Carefully inspect clothing for flaws and stains. Take them out into the daylight if they are in a dark garage. Plug in appliances to try them if possible. Bring assorted batteries with you to test battery-operated items like radios and toys.

Take a gamble. Garage sales items are typically at pennies on the dollar compared to new. Allow yourself to make some mistakes yet still enjoy considerable savings. Reasonable gambles include estimating clothing sizes for children for a future school year, or hoping decorator towels for fifty cents match your bathroom wallpaper.

Don't forget that what you buy will never look less worn or in better condition than the day you buy it. Don't buy their "junk" to bring home to be your "junk." Do you really need a doughnut fryer? I already mentioned my garlic roaster. It was new and in its original box. Maybe that should have been a clue. I used it a few times and then it took up valuable cupboard space. A few months after I bought it, I learned how to roast garlic by wrapping it in foil. I donated the garlic roaster and moved on. A good deal still isn't a good deal if it isn't something you really need. Be careful out there.

Finally, be open to surprises and enjoy. My mother-in-law has found new designer clothes with tags still on them for her grandchildren. One of my daughters found a toy microphone in a neighbor's freebie box. It has been a popular toy at our house for over three years. I have had great luck with toys, furniture, clothing, and kitchen items.

Bragging about the deals you find or quietly smiling and accepting the compliment on your "new" designer dress is part of the fun. You may find surprises and treasures out there too. Happy hunting!

If you have children and want to garage sale hunt:

It is a hot summer day. The kids would rather be anywhere but riding around in a hot car looking for garage sales. Here are tips to make it bearable and fun for everyone.

- Keep children amused and fed while riding in the car. Plan for a garage sale excursion like a regular road trip. Bring munchies and activities to keep them content between stops.

- Limit the length of garage sale outings. Be realistic. No one likes to drive around in a hot car and constantly get in and out.

- Let the kids have spending money to make their own purchases. It is an inexpensive way to give them practice making purchasing decisions. It also helps teach them math and communication skills. Many garage sales now have toy freebie boxes so Mom can shop longer without distraction.

- Or, if you know your kids really won't enjoy the outing consider hiring a babysitter to let the kids frolic at home, especially if you discover you like to go hunting regularly. You may more than make up the cost of a sitter with your garage sale bargains!

- Think ahead for kid toys, clothing, and sporting equipment. Kids outgrow this stuff before they wear it out, especially in the smaller sizes. Thoughtful buys include raincoats, ice skates, roller skates and bicycles.

- Many plastic toys can be scrubbed or possibly even run through the dishwasher to clean them — upper rack only and check the type of plastic to be sure it won't melt! Many stuffed animals still have tags or you may decide the price is good enough that you are willing to find out if it will survive a trip through your washer and dryer (Be sure your washer and dryer can handle this too. Check the manuals).

- Don't give up on toys with missing or broken parts. Replace parts by ordering them from the original manufacturer. Call 1-800-555-1212 to see if a company has a toll free customer service number or check the Internet. The number for Little Tikes is 1-800-321-0183. The Fisher Price number is 1-800-432-5437. (This doesn't just apply to toy manufacturers. I received free replacement cookie press patterns from the manufacturer when I lost mine last Christmas.)

CHAPTER 13

HAVE A GARAGE SALE: TURN CLUTTER INTO CASH

Garage sale signs in spring are sort of like Christmas lights in December. Whether you like to shop the sales, hold the sales, or do both, consider Carla's thoughts for turning household clutter into cash. I consulted my friend and garage sale guru Carla for her tips on having a garage sale. Carla likes to have garage sales for fun, sharing stories with people, and turning clutter in her house into cash in her hand. She once held a two-day sale with friends that generated over $1,400. This was especially impressive when she explained that there were only three "expensive" items at the sale (items in the $50 to $100 range). Most items sold for under $10. I was impressed.

Carla's background in marketing helps her think like a retailer when it comes to marketing garage sale stuff. Here are Carla's suggestions for marketing, merchandising, pricing, and handling the money at a garage sale:

1. Location, location, location: Hold your sale on a busy high traffic street. Carla recommends having a sale with friends for fun and to share the work. Have the sale at the house on the busiest street. It will be worth the extra effort to haul your stuff there.
2. Pick the right time to have a sale. Carla suggests May and June, instead of later in the summer when more people are away on vacation.
3. Combine your sale with other sales: Have a block sale or a neighborhood sale. Multiple sales draw more customers.
4. Advertise in your local paper. Locals know the area and

have a better chance to find you.

5. Use signs to simply point the way. Use large signs on bright colored poster board. Many people try to put too much tiny print and information on their signs that can't be read as people drive by. Carla suggests signs that simply say "Sale" with an arrow to point the way. Put signs out only during the dates and times of the sale. Don't list merchandise or worry about including your address on the sign — people just want to get to the sale, and they may not know the area well enough to be helped by an address.

6. Put items out on the driveway going all the way out to the street to lure people to your sale. If you have a small sale, put everything on the driveway so it looks like as much as possible.

7. Put a "Free Stuff" box out on the end of the driveway with a large sign to draw in customers.

8. Place an inexpensive "toy" box by the checkout just outside of the garage. Kids can browse there while parents shop in the garage and everybody wins.

9. Put small trays of jewelry or other small items by the checkout for people to browse while they wait to get checked out.

10. Be ready to start as soon as you open your garage door. People won't wait for you to be ready. Tuck items under tables in the driveway the night before so that you can haul them out quickly and easily without interfering with people who want to shop the garage tables right away.

Carla's merchandising tips

- Put everything out if you have space. Don't hold back things you think won't sell. Carla is often amazed at what sells first. It is often the stuff you think no one would ever buy.

- Sell clean merchandise. Take the time to dust and wash

items. Make things look like new merchandise being sold at a great price.

- Include instruction manuals and original boxes with merchandise when possible.
- Organize your merchandise like a retailer. Group things together. Create categories like: Christmas items, toys, stuffed animals, hardware, kitchen utensils.
- Use cardboard box lids to make trays for jewelry and small collectibles. Use small plastic zip-top bags for things that come in pieces, hair holders, and small items in categories to sell as a group like baby rattles or match box cars.
- Consider renting 6ft to 8ft banquet trestle tables for as little as $10 to $14 for three days. It makes setting up a lot easier and it is worth the minimal expense.
- Have an extension cord available so people can check out electrical items.
- Take the time to straighten up the tables and keep things looking orderly and nice.

Pricing is critical

- Price everything. Many people are basically shy at a sale and won't bother to ask the price if they don't see one.
- Pre-price items with non-residue masking tape because it won't get too gummy or leave a tacky mark.
- Use big price tags with descriptions for big items. They are easier to see and help prevent any "swapping." People can purchase an item just by grabbing the tag rather than hauling a large item up to you.
- Set up big items or items that come in pieces, like tents, paddling pools, or exercise equipment. If this is too tedious, bring the box with the pieces and tape a photo of the assembled item to the box so people can see what it looks like.
- If an item is too heavy or bulky to bring to the sale, bring

several photocopied sheets showing a photo, description, price, and your phone number. This works well for large furniture. Carla sold her car this way.

- Price items fairly and realistically. If you price things too high, people may leave or take up too much of your time with dickering. If people dicker in front of other people at the sale, it opens the door for more dickering.

- Don't dicker the first day of the sale unless it is an item you really want to sell. Consider letting people know it is the first day and asking them to come back tomorrow to dicker if the item hasn't sold by then.

- If people come up with an armload of stuff and want to dicker on everything, ask if you can total everything and then knock off a percentage for them. This is faster, and it indicates to others standing nearby that you are willing to offer a volume discount but you aren't opening the door to argue about the price of each and every item for everyone at the sale.

- Be loud and clear that you will dicker on the second day. On the second day, let people know when they walk up that you are ready to bargain and no reasonable offer will be refused.

- At the end of the sale, box up what hasn't sold. Make arrangements prior to the sale for a charity to come pick up unsold items the day after the sale. Take the tax write-off for these things.

Safe & Simplified Money Handling

Carla shared a heart-breaking story of a friend who had made several hundred dollars at her garage sale and then had the cash box disappear at the end of the last day.

Here are her suggestions for handling the money:

- Price items in rounded increments for easy adding at the checkout: 25 cents, 50 cents, 75 cents, $1. It is also helpful to have a printing calculator that runs a print-out tape when people purchase many items.

- Start with about $100 float for making change – $10 in coins, $30 in singles, and the rest in five-dollar bills.
- Keep the coins in a box at the table, but use a zipped money belt for the cash, so you don't have to worry about walking away from the cash table.
- Use a cookie sheet to quickly put price stickers on at the checkout. Sort out whose sales are whose later, not while your customers wait in line.
- Don't let people put an item on "hold" unless you have cash or check in hand. Let them pay upfront and collect the item later if they need to bring their car round to the sale.
- Don't accept checks as payment, but do accept them as a deposit to trade for cash when people return later to pick up big-ticket items.

CHAPTER 14

CONSUMERISM DOESN'T CLEAR CLUTTER

Most of us admit we live in a consumption-oriented materialistic society. The frightening part is the way this underlying attitude has permeated every aspect of our American lives. We spend our work time earning money to pay for goods. We spend our leisure time shopping for new toys that are marketed to us under the pretense that they will make our lives simpler and happier, and we spend much of our remaining time maintaining these new toys. When are we going to figure out a better way to live?

A friend of mine who had just helped run a garage sale observed an interesting trend. She said sales attendance wasn't down, but the volume of purchases was down. Lots of people were walking up and looking, but fewer were buying. Since garage sale items are so reasonably priced, she thought it odd that people wouldn't grab things for a quarter or fifty cents just to try them. She hoped maybe the thoughts of the simplicity movement were finally taking hold.

I am not so sure. Is it possible that we are all simply reaching a saturation point with the quantity of stuff in our lives?

I was recently in a home that was overflowing with stuff. There were clever knick-knacks in the family room, every lotion, spray, and whatnot in the bathroom, books crammed onto bookshelves that reflected 20 years of reading trends. All this stuff could not possibly be currently in use. Did bringing it home in the first place help? Will bringing home more make life in this house better?

Unknown to my family, I had been thinking about getting a

kitten. In a weird dream one night, I was buying a new kitten. The problem in my dream was this: there were three kittens that I liked and I wanted all three. "More is better" even in my dreams? In my dream, I eventually decided to purchase just my first pick and to let the other two go. When I woke up, I realized we already owned two neglected dogs, and I decided my time could be used best spending more time with our current pets. Maybe I was shopping for love when it was already right under my nose. Certainly more animal hair, food dishes, and veterinarian bills weren't going to improve our life.

It is amazingly easy in our society to run out and grab "more." I find it takes constant effort to force myself to stay put and spend time with what I already have. Why is it more fun to shop for a new kitten than to play with the family pets I already have? Why is it more fun to shop for new windows than to clean the dirty ones we already own? Why is it more fun to buy new clothes than to sew a button back on something already in my closet?

We have been taught that shopping is fun and easy. We can simply buy something to make our lives happier. We collectively follow the path of least resistance as we head out the door and throw our plastic on the counter at the checkout. We eventually become vaguely frustrated as we struggle to pay bills, wade through our clutter, and work overtime to pay off our debt.

I will not enjoy a new acquisition as much as I do when I am on the hunt for it. Once I buy "it," I have to worry about paying for it. I have to store "it." I have to take care of "it." And, "it," whatever it is, doesn't stay new or in style once I bring it home. Once I have "it" home, I learn its flaws—it isn't quite the right color, or size, or it doesn't work as well as I thought it would. Many purchases are designed to be disposable simply so we will need to head out soon to buy more.

The economy is sometimes uncertain. I remind myself daily of my 99-year-old grandfather's advice: "Play it close to the belt.

Don't go into debt."

To his advice I add: "Direct your energy to the people, pets, and finally things that you already have, rather than heading out the door in search of more."

CHAPTER 15

DAILY PAPER CLUTTER

Paper clutter: magazines, newspapers, newsletters, announcements, bills, statements, invitations, and income tax documents. All this and more can add up to moving piles of paper, paper clutter, and too much time spent hunting for, sorting, and organizing household paperwork. How can I get rid of paper clutter and get my paperwork organized?

Here are some points to keep in mind. Deal with paper daily. Paper attacks daily. It arrives by mail. It comes home from work. Our children bring it to us in their backpacks. Don't let it build up. It doesn't take as long to go through the mail as you think it does. Spend ten minutes per day to deal with mail and other paperwork. Set the timer in your kitchen for ten minutes. The time will go quickly and you'll feel better afterwards. Honest.

Put the junk mail and the unimportant stuff you know you won't have time to read into the recycle bin. Remember the 80-20 rule? It applies to paper too. You will retrieve less than 20 per cent of what you file in your long-term household filing system, so think hard before you save something to file just because you might read it or need it "some day." That day rarely arrives.

In addition to recycling paperwork, you are tossing the guilt you feel every time you walk by the unread pile of magazines perched on the table. Yes, you "paid good money" for that subscription, but it isn't doing you any good. Instead, it is actually making you feel bad. Feel bad once as you donate or recycle that stuff. Toss the guilt.

Make a date with yourself to file paperwork once per week in your household filing system. If you do it weekly, it probably won't take more than fifteen minutes to get things sorted and filed. Sort and file in a way that is logical for you. There is no one right way to organize and file.

Keep your paperwork system simple. Create one system and stick with it. Disorganization happens when we have multiple systems going. Think about where you have business cards and phone numbers. Maybe you have some business cards and phone numbers tacked onto the refrigerator, some tucked in a kitchen drawer, and some stuffed in an address book somewhere. That's really three systems. That's three places to have to hunt when you are looking for one phone number!

Handling paperwork is a process. I get a little crabby at paper experts who say to handle each piece of paper only once. Maybe you need to consult with other family members when an invitation or event appears. Maybe you just aren't ready to make an instant decision on attending the party or signing up for the class the second you open the mail. I think a successful paperwork system must take real life into consideration. Consider a two-stage system. Stage one is for daily paper, and stage two is your long-term household filing system.

Daily paperwork requires a simple system located where it will be used. This means a small daily system apart from the long-term storage file cabinet. Keep the system small and simple for you. Don't copy my system or any other organizing "expert's" system. If your paperwork management system isn't tailored to you and your life, you won't trust it and you won't use it.

Put your paperwork system where you will use it. If you have to run to a basement office several times a day to deal with everyday paperwork, it won't happen. For many people, this means creating a small working system in the kitchen because that is where paper often seems to pile. It can be on a shelf with the cookbooks, in a kitchen drawer or cupboard, or up above the cupboards if your cabinets don't go all the way to the ceiling.

Group similar categories of paper together every day. One way to do this would be to have a few folders in the kitchen. Use one folder for bills and other paper that needs to get filed weekly into the long-term filing system, a pending folder for upcoming events – shows, weddings, practice schedules, meeting schedules, and possibly, a folder for each family member – especially children so their school information is handy if you need to check on something. Keep it simple. Make it fit the way you really live your life and the way your home is laid out.

Beat the Junk Mail & Credit Card Offer Blues

A large part of the daily paper pile comes right in the door with us every day. I am talking about the mail. If we can get rid of extra mail before it even comes into our house, we can reduce the paper clutter we have to throw away. Maybe we can even save a few trees in the process.

Go to: www.dmachoice.org and www.obviously.com/junk mail/ for paper and email reduction ideas.

If you are tired of the numerous credit card offers and pre-approved cards that come in the mail every week, call the number below for the Opt Out Request Line. Registering with the Opt Out Request Line tells the credit bureaus that they no longer have permission to sell your name and financial data to the banks and financial companies that send you all those credit card offers. You will need to have your name, address, and Social Security number handy.

If you stay on the phone and listen to all the options, there is a choice to "opt out" permanently. The Opt Out Request Line will send a form in the mail that you sign and send back. Remember, if "permanent" sounds scary and you miss the credit card offers, you can call them back. I bet I am down to two or three credit offers per year now!

The Opt Out Request Line for Experion, Novus, Equifax, and TransUnion is: 1-888-567-8688. Or go to their website at www.optoutprescreen.com.

Finally, tax time is coming. Tax time will come every year.

One simple way to keep taxes organized is to create a tax file for the year at the start of the year. Now is not too late. Throughout the year, put any documents you will need at tax time in this folder, including charitable donations, license tab renewals, education expenses, business expenses, and income received. This will save a lot of stress and time wasted hunting for tax preparation paperwork.

Paperwork is a process that won't go away. My suggestions are to deal with it daily, file weekly, toss (recycle) as much of the paperwork and guilt as you can as soon and as often as you can, and, finally, create a single simple system that is uniquely yours.

CHAPTER 16

"MOVING PILES" OF PAPER CLUTTER

I don't want to get too personal, but do you occasionally suffer from "moving piles" and other paper clutter? Moving piles are piles of paper that land on the kitchen counter and then travel around to other flat surfaces in your kitchen or home.

When you want to make dinner, you move the current pile or piles from the counter to the dinner table. When you want to set the dinner table, you move the piles from the dinner table to a living room or dining room table. After dinner, so you don't forget to deal with this paperwork, you put the piles back into the kitchen. You are then ready for the dance to begin again. And again.

Paper clutter afflicts many households. The bottom line is paper clutter or "moving piles" are basically mobile stacks of indecision. Not knowing what to do with that article, invitation, or mail offer, you keep moving it around. Personally, I don't have this problem completely licked yet. I usually do have a small "working pile" on the corner of my own kitchen counter. Real life isn't perfect.

Paperwork is easier to deal with when I try to keep my quantity of unmade decisions fairly small and under control. Since paperwork piles are unmade decisions, I try to get better, faster, and smarter at making paperwork decisions. Here are some tips to help conquer those daily "moving piles" and to keep them from growing out of control.

I ask myself a few questions to clarify if I will ever need a piece of paper again. What would be the worst thing that would happen if I tossed it? If I can live with the answer, I might not need to keep the paper. I also ask: How hard would it be to get this information again if I decide I need it later? Could I call the school, or a friend, or look it up on the Internet?

Next, I try to reward myself for making these decisions. I promise myself a treat for dealing with the paper clutter, and then I follow through with it. This could mean a stop to the coffee shop or the ice cream parlor! Rewards are especially helpful for dealing with a backlog of paperwork, like cleaning out old files in file cabinets that are crammed full.

If you are afraid to file something because you might not find it again, consider these ideas. If the system is simple, small, and tailored to you, you will be able to trust and use it. Also, consider creating a system that still lets you see all this paper work. Instead of folders tucked away in a kitchen drawer, try a more visible and open system. Put hanging baskets on the kitchen wall or magnetized baskets on the side of the refrigerator, so you can still see the top edges of all of the papers. Or, use folders but keep them out in a visible open "stacking" tray system.

Whatever ideas you use to beat those "moving piles," make the system work for you and fit your own lifestyle. Remember, there is no one right way to do it. Choose what fits for you!

CHAPTER 17

ORGANIZE LONG-TERM PAPER

The 80-20 rule of paperwork still taunts me. I know I will not retrieve 80 per cent of what I have filed, yet when I look back through the paperwork, I am reminded of parts of my life I have forgotten. I laugh at a fictional short story I wrote back in college. I don't understand the goals in an old performance review from a previous employer. I enjoy re-reading special cards and notes from old friends. I am not ready to get rid of it all, but it is time to enjoy the memories and to weed it down.

Because of my interest in simple living, people sometimes think I am in favor of "pitching it all." I am not. It is okay to be a "saver," if you set up your filing system so that you can retrieve, enjoy, and use your information when you want it. Frankly, if a filing system isn't functional for its owner, then the filed paper might as well have been recycled instead of saved.

Here are ideas for tweaking your long-term filing system:

First, gather all paper of a particular type into one location. I'm infamous for tucking away related paperwork tidbits in many different spots — a craft article in a nightstand, a related magazine in a bathroom "reading" basket, a piece more in a kitchen drawer, and a pile in a labeled folder in my file cabinet. I can't weed it down or organize it until I've gathered it all together.

Second, if there is paperwork you know you don't really need but you have trouble parting with it, think about why this is the case. If the information means something to you, maybe you could save a few representative samples and journal about the rest. If not, try to get "sentimental" and "historical" information out of the regular household files by creating separate folders for them: you could label them "Special cards," "High School Memories," or "Previous Jobs." The goal is to preserve the memories without clogging the filing system. On a rather morbid note, I think about my children having to go through all of this stuff some day.

Third, review your file labels. Your life changes over time, so your filing categories need to be updated too. The only filing constant is that categories will change, so I label files in pencil! Sometimes a folder gets too thick despite my efforts to weed it out, so I create two folders with the same label followed by a numeric designation. In other cases, it is time to create two slightly different file categories and sort my paperwork a little more specifically. My bulging "Travel" folder turned into "Minnesota Travel" and "Outstate Travel" Sometimes I also use several "mini" categories or smaller folders (8 1/2"x11") within a legal-size (11"x14") folder. My large folder might be "Insurance" and within it could be sub-folders for the house, auto, and life insurance.

Fourth, create wiggle room and "spare" folders: Household filing isn't an exact science. I like to have enough extra space in each file drawer to allow easy filing and wiggle room. I also like to keep a few extra folders and file labels on hand to accommodate life changes like new hobbies or interests. This may sound like common sense, but for me, it encourages better filing behavior and it prevents me from just shoving new information into a drawer or piling it on a desktop. Any pile can become a file.

Finally, I would like to share my two cents on cross-referencing and indexing. For years, I thought either topic was overkill in a discussion about household paperwork. That was my opinion before I conducted a frantic search for a piece of paper that turned out to be in a safety deposit box and before I had three different folders in my cabinet that all contained the same kind of information under different headings. Cross-referencing can be as simple as putting a piece of paper in the "Insurance" file that says a certain document is in the "Vehicle" file. Indexing can be as simple as a list at the front of your filing system that shows all the folder labels (If I had indexed sooner, I wouldn't have had these three folders: "Christmas Crafts," "Holiday Ideas," and "Seasonal Activities.").

Try a paper management book to get ideas and to help keep you motivated for this tedious task. I am a fan of: *Taming the Paper Tiger* by Barbara Hemphill, and *The Office Clutter Cure* by Don Aslett, and *File Don't Pile* by Pat Dorff.

I don't want to be overly zealous about household paperwork. Spring is short. I just want to save time for things that are more fun than hours spent frantically hunting for a piece of paper.

CHAPTER 18

PURGE LONG-TERM PAPER CLUTTER

Paper. Paper. Paper. It is probably the Number #1 form of household clutter for many of us. It is hard to decide where to put paper when it arrives. It is even harder to decide to weed paper out once it has nested in our home filing system.

It was time for me to weed out our household files. It was getting harder and harder to wedge additional incoming paperwork into our overflowing file cabinet. I couldn't figure out how four people managed to fill four deep file drawers with routine household paperwork! What happened to clutter clearing?

I worked at weeding out our paperwork for several days. I finally had a combined paperwork pile that stood about 18" tall that was ready for the shredder and the recycle bag. I am embarrassed that someone who promotes the "simple life" could come up with that much excess paper, but there was a sense of accomplishment in measuring the stack at the end. And, truth be told, I suspect I am still hanging on to more paper than we really need.

Weeding out paperwork was hard. I was plagued by uncertainty as I held each piece of paper from each file folder in my hands. Would I "need" it again? Was it "safe" to toss it? The decision making process wore me out. Read on to see what I learned.

Keep a pad and pencil handy.

Jot down the different types of paperwork that you are afraid to toss as you go through your files. Credit card statements? Receipts? Utility bills? Paycheck stubs? Write your uncertainty down. *Take this list to ask your tax person or accountant or call your government tax help phone line when the next tax session rolls around. Take notes on what the person tells you. You will suffer from less uncertainty next time you weed out your paperwork. It would probably be wise to do this regularly since tax laws change over time.*

Have a stapler handy.

I found way too many wads of related papers that were paper clipped together. Shame on me. Paper clips are dangerous. They can fall off. Worse yet, they can snag other papers that then become lost. Weed out the paper clips and staple related papers together. Also, have a staple remover handy too! Go and buy one if you don't have this as part of your household office supplies.

Create a pile for misfiled papers and sort the paper clutter.

I found misfiled items, so resolve to be ready for a few misfiled papers at the onset, just in case. I also sorted the discarded papers into two piles – those that needed to be shredded and those that could just be recycled.

Work in small increments of time.

I personally suggest working for no more than 15 minutes to an hour at a crack. Tackle only a few file folders at a time. Also, do this work in your personal prime time if you can. Why? Because it is hard to sit and make decision after decision. As you get tired of it, there is a strong temptation to skip files or wads of paper that you think probably are "good enough." In this case, doing less at a time will add up to getting rid of more paper clutter.

Consider going through the whole process twice in a row.

What?! Yep, you heard me. After you have gone through each file once, consolidated files, deleted files, and created new ones, you can be more confident about your decision-making. You will find more to weed out if you go through a second round while you are up on this process. It was worth the effort, and it went much faster the second time anyway.

Shred in the dark.

Shred statements and other paperwork that has personal data on it in the dark or while watching television. Why? If you don't, you may find yourself second-guessing yourself as you slow down to look at what you are trying to get rid of. Trust yourself. You already made the decisions. (If you really do feel the need to double-check everything, be my guest. You are the best judge of your own situation.)

Finally, when you are done, reward yourself! Paper clutter is piles of unmade decisions and you just made a whole bunch of them! When it was all said and done, I found it to be an empowering experience. I now know a lot more about what I have, and I love the "extra" space that now exists between the files. Oh, dear... Have I made future filing easier or have I created the potential for new interests or hobbies to enter my life because I now have file space for them?

CHAPTER 19

PHOTO CLUTTER – PHOTOS, PHOTOS, & MORE UNSORTED PHOTOS

One of my favorite childhood memories was seeing the picture frame on Dad's bedroom dresser that held annual pictures of me arranged from kindergarten through high school. It was a childhood ritual for me to walk back to my parents' bedroom with Dad when he'd get home from work to tell him about my school day while he'd get ready to change before dinner. I think seeing those pictures so carefully mark my progress through life told me how much my parents cared for me.

When I mention unsorted photographs as a clutter issue in my simple living classes, there is almost always collective eye rolling and groaning in the room. According to time management author Ronni Eisenberg in *The Overwhelmed Person's Guide to Time Management,* unsorted photos are in the top three of people's undone household projects.

Most of us know what we are "supposed" to do with all those photos: develop them or print them promptly, sort them, label them right away, and display them quickly in frames and photo-safe albums or scrapbooks, and send others, as promised, to friends or family. To earn gold stars here, we also know it is a good idea to store negatives or digital CDs or DVDs off site, perhaps in a safety deposit box. Many of us, including me, fall behind somewhere in this process. Some of us are also dealing with multiple medias—old photos and negatives and new digital photos and storage systems.

In the past, I have scanned quickly through a new packet of photos while sitting in the car or standing at the kitchen counter. Next, I shoved all of them (the good, the bad, and the fuzzy) back into the envelope they came in, and tossed them on top of a growing pile of photo packets. This hasn't worked out so well.

Maybe part of the problem is there are too many photo options out there. If starting an album or scrapbook, what kind will it be? A family album, a vacation album, a Christmas album, an album for each child, an annual album? Or, consider high-tech possibilities: digital photos, scanned photos, photos at a website, or photos on CDs. Think about display choices: the size, number, and kinds of picture frames out there too.

If you display part of your large family, do you need to have a picture for everyone? Do you want all the frames to match? What size(s) would work best? Do you have to go back to make enlargements every time? Do you want to make nail holes in the walls or to move pictures on tables and dressers every time you dust? How many copies do you need? Who are you "supposed" to send copies? No wonder some of us wind up stuffing photos back into their packets and adding them to a growing pile.

If unsorted photos are a backburner dilemma at your house, you are not alone and a few small changes may make some big improvements for you. There are some simple steps that can improve the photo process and give you some peace of mind. Work on learning a couple of photo sorting habits (yes, I said the "h" word again). You pick which new habit(s) would help you. Check out the following suggestions.

Toss or delete bad photos the first time you go through them. Immediately toss any photos that are blurry, too dark, too light, or missing somebody's body part (usually the top of someone's head). Why would you want to store these in any format for years and years?

Next, make it a habit to date each photo right away — be kind to yourself here, an approximate date is fine most of the time, for example September 2000. In ten years, who will care if the first day of school was September 7th or September 8th?

Starting with the photos you take this week, get into the habit of displaying them in frames, albums, or scrapbooks right away. Put them up on a corkboard. Enjoy them! Don't worry about the backlog yet. Just try to capture the present and move forward. Scrapbooks are nice because you can record the written story that goes with the picture before you forget. Remember, scrapbook pages do not have to be decorated for hours and hours unless this is your personal choice for a hobby.

Try to pick one or two photo display processes for yourself and stick with them. If you go in too many directions at once, you won't be able to keep up. For example, don't try to start a vacation album, an album for each child, and an annual family album all at once. When I tried that approach, I wound up with several partial albums and little stacks of photos sitting around. If that doesn't sound too bad, I also confess that the little stacks didn't have labels on them to remind me which albums they were supposed to go in.

Label packets of photos by jotting down approximate dates and brief notes of what's in each packet ("Christmas and Easter 2007"). Store them chronologically in a safe place. If you don't have time to do more than this, at least things will be in order and ready for you at a later date. Allow room for expansion. Consider how many rolls you take annually. I really don't want to confess how many times I "organized" my photo packets somewhere in my house, only to run out of room a few months or years down the road.

Finally, tackle the photo backlog. It won't take as long as you think it will. You may have spent years creating the backlog. You also probably spent years worrying about it off and on. It won't take years to take care of it. In a few hours, days, or weeks you can have that backlog on its way to being resolved or at least vastly improved, and it will feel like a weight has been lifted from your shoulders. You will be rewarded for your effort. You will unearth some wonderful gems in the process. You will find some great pictures in there — things that may make you laugh or cry.

Photos can help awaken our memories and in doing that, they can give us great perspective by reminding us of our earlier selves, friends, and family. They provide each of us with a personal history and give continuity to our life. Change a few simple "processing" habits to prevent unsorted photographs from going to waste. You can do it, and if you keep it simple, it won't take as long as you think it will.

~

Section 3
Summer

~

CHAPTER 1

LAWN FURNITURE CLUTTER—MAYBE

Simplify your outdoor entertaining with beautiful lawn furniture that is fashionable yet classic, detailed yet easy to maintain, and sturdy yet convenient to store. Wow your friends and family with your effortless outdoor parties and your terrific outdoor furnishings! It is just that easy if you buy all the right stuff, right?

"Outdoor living rooms" are supposed to be all the rage right now. But I'm not buying it. Do "they" forget where some of us live? Thunderstorms, pollen, humidity, bugs, dirt, and the shortness of the summer season all take their toll on our Minnesota outdoor guests and furnishings. Yet, I too have succumbed to the visions of a backyard that looks like it is straight from a landscape magazine.

When my family moved into our first home, I conducted careful research and purchased (for more money than I'm willing to admit) many pieces of fine enamel-coated steel outdoor furniture from a well-known manufacturer. Our deck was over-crowded with furniture before my husband had even finished construction. And, I will not even discuss the problems of where to store and stack all this stuff for the other nine months of the year.

Over the years, the enamel chipped, the steel rusted, and the thick cushions mildewed and became stained. The glass-topped tables rarely looked clean. I learned how much "fun" it was to sit on cushions that looked dry but still had water in them from the rain two days ago. Our large round glass-topped table took numerous trips across the deck when strong winds caught the umbrella that had been left open. Winter shoveling around these pieces was no fun either.

Something had to be done. There had to be a better solution.

I began to eliminate pieces that were wrecked or never used. It turned out that many charities have zero interest in rusty old lawn furniture. We finally gave up and used the city dump. I solemnly vowed not to repeat my mistakes. And yet, 15 years later I began to look longingly again at lawn furniture.

Where trendy styles and fabrics couldn't hook me in, new technology did. I have gone from an expensive 12-piece set to four folding sling chairs and a mesh-topped metal table. This time everything was purchased for under $200. The chairs are nylon mesh rather than cushions so they won't retain water. The metal on everything is now "powder coated" which is more durable and less prone to rust. And best of all, everything (even the table) folds for convenient storage during the rest of the year.

I didn't know what color to get. I knew I didn't want clear glass table tops because the tops and undersides of them never stayed clean. My old white furniture showed the rust horribly, yet sometimes white can hide more dirt than darker colors.

Never mind. I was ready for a change.

The table is a black metal with a metal mesh top, and the metal chair frames and plastic arm rests are dark green. After all the pollen we had the first spring, I began to be sorry, but then I realized my regret was outweighed by the pleasure of looking at something new after 15 years!

Maybe that's the problem. The first time I purchased deck furniture, I wanted it to "last forever." The reality is that stuff doesn't last (especially outdoor furniture in Minnesota) and in any case, I enjoy change. Maybe the trick is to let stuff flow through my life rather than let it get stuck out on my deck for 15 years.

CHAPTER 2

UNCLUTTER SUMMER YARD WORK

When we moved to our first home many years ago, it was the year of the drought. "Experts" advised people to let the lawns go dormant. For us, unfortunately, almost half of it died. As enthusiastic first-time homeowners, we were determined to bring it back. Maybe that was a mistake.

Little landscaping had been done to our yard before we moved in. While we revived the lawn with youthful energy and enthusiasm, we also planted trees and shrubs, landscaped and added a garden. In short, we created a lot of yard work for ourselves — mowing, trimming, planting, weeding, and raking were a few of the new pastimes we happily assumed.

Now a hectic summer schedule regularly competes with my vision of idyllic "lazy summer days." By mid-June, my passion for keeping up with the yard work has already waned. Some people enjoy yard work. They call it gardening and they see it as a relaxing hobby or a quiet communion with nature. I don't. Heat, humidity, gnats, and mosquitoes nibble away at my enthusiasm for yard work. Weeds crop up unchecked. Potted plants grow limp from lack of watering, and the grass, though nice and green, grows faster than I can find the time to cut it. Somehow I still have the audacity to want an attractive and enjoyable yard, but I admit I am lazy.

Simplifying yard work has been an ongoing process of trial and error for me. I am very much a work in progress. Here is where I stand with mowing, weeding and maintaining the yard as a pleasant environment to relax in.

I finally learned to follow some of my own clutter habits advice with regard to lawn mowing. I finally made mowing a habit. I cut the grass regularly instead of "when it needs it." When the grass is growing fast, I mow the lawn on Mondays and Thursdays. There are several advantages to this system. I don't get rained out as often and wind up with hay. I don't fret over my yard every time I see it and wonder if it is time to mow. I now know when I will mow, and I rarely have to bag the grass. It doesn't get long enough to need bagging, so I can mow my yard faster. I also decided to enjoy this activity — it really is an opportunity for me to take a solitary (though not quiet) walk around my yard. Why did I used to complain that I had to mow?

Weeding is another story. Stooping, bending, wrenching, pulling, and perspiring are not favorite pastimes of mine. Instead, I fell hopelessly in love with mulch. Mulch is multipurpose. It holds moisture in the soil and dramatically reduces weeds. The weeds I do find are easier to pull because they are often just loosely growing in the mulch instead of deeply anchored in the soil. Another thing I finally learned about weeding is that if I stay on top of this task, it takes only a few minutes to weed. This is time better spent than walking by the weeds, staring at them, and feeling bad, time after time. I now quickly yank weeds out the first time I spot them, when they are little, and before they have a chance to bother me, grow, or multiply. It only takes a moment.

General yard work can also be simplified by owning the right tools — another case of having the best tools for the job. Over time, I have become a huge fan of quality equipment. I like hoses that are long enough and won't crack. I gloat over sprinklers with timers. I thrill to a freshly sharpened lawn mower blade or a decent rake. Shoulder straps that help save my back are a must. It is awful to struggle with yard work with poor equipment. Do I go so far as to say that decent tools can actually make yard work enjoyable? Maybe so. Certainly less tiring.

But I still can't say "enjoyable" about gardening, because I am just not a gardener. For a few years I tried.

One year I accidentally planted enough lettuce to feed the entire neighborhood. The next year my green beans turned out great, but my family reminded me that even though I could grow them, they still didn't like this vegetable. Wasted effort. Another year I disgusted my children with broccoli with little green worms on it. Other years included too many tomatoes and peppers that just didn't do well for some mysterious reason.

I did learn to take gardening notes from year to year, so I wouldn't keep repeating my mistakes. It took me years to make my peace with the fact that I wasn't enjoying the process anyway.

To be honest with ourselves and not ascribe to society's "shoulds" and "ought to's" is a clutter clearing goal that can be applied to our yards and gardens. My vegetable garden now consists of raspberry bushes, rhubarb, and lots of mulch.

I guess I sometimes am a slow learner. I now content myself with better mowing habits, mulch, good tools, and regular trips to the local farmer's market.

CHAPTER 3

CHILDREN UNCLUTTER MY LIFE
– NO KIDDING!

After a few years of parenting, I decided my children could help unclutter my life. No, I hadn't lost it. Bear with me a minute. Think of it this way: Busy, stressed out parents need a break now and then, and their children need to learn responsibility and be introduced to nurturing others too. I am talking about chores. It's that simple.

Simple living is about balance, so it follows that part of family balance includes balancing out household chores. If my husband and I make dinner, our kids clear the table and load the dishwasher. (Don't you remember the days when *you* were the dishwasher?) Now the adults get a turn to relax and visit.

DELEGATE

When I mow the yard, my kids pull weeds. Sometimes I pay them a penny per weed. Sometimes I don't. We all use the yard. We can all work to take care of it. My youngest child has the job of being my "spotter" when I tour the yard with a shovel to clean up after the dogs. The kids also feed and walk the dogs.

When company is coming, my kids vacuum and dust while I clean the bathrooms. If I am busy and they are hungry, they go make their own breakfast or lunch. They can handle it. They gain valuable experience when they handle it.

If you are past the point of having kids in your home, or if you didn't have them in the first place, look around you for this young and eager work force. Consider nieces, nephews, friends' children, grandchildren, and enterprising neighborhood children to simplify yard work or other household tasks.

In an age of convenience, gadgets, and commercialism, we've forgotten the inexpensive/free labor force sitting right under our own noses. It is time to build character, teach responsibility, and enjoy the fruits of *their* labors.

TRAIN THEM UP

I learned (the hard way) that training on chores is necessary and it is my parental responsibility. I figured I could tell kids to "go tidy up your room" and they would sort and organize the way I, as an adult, would do it. After finding building blocks mixed in with shoes and game pieces intermixed in boxes, I slowly learned. I discovered time spent training them has big paybacks later. And I've dropped some of my perfectionism. If I want cheerful willing help, I had better not scream if the completed task isn't quite up to my usual standard.

FIND HIDDEN REWARDS

There were hidden rewards during this household chore balancing process at our house. The kids and I discovered that we enjoy folding laundry together. We get chatty. The laundry gets done three times faster. Bam! It's done. One person is not stuck with doing it all, and before long, we are all on to more entertaining things. I really dislike folding laundry. Now there is help and cheerful company!

EXPLORE PARENTING RESOURCES

I am not an intuitive parent who automatically knows what my kids can do to help at what ages. There is help for that too. Too many parenting books to read can be anything but simplifying. Parenting books can give contradictory advice or just make us play the "I'm not a good enough parent..." tape in our heads. Feel free to skip them and do what fits for your family. But I found these books helpful.

Pick Up Your Socks by Elizabeth Crary is one place to start. She discusses what tasks are appropriate at which ages.

I am also a fan of *Raising Self-Reliant Children in a Self-Indulgent World* by H. Stephen Glenn & Jane Nelsen. The title is self-explanatory. *Kiplinger's Money-Smart Kids* by Janet Bodnar is a resource on the related topic of allowances and how they can be used.

ACCEPT NURTURING

This is the "nurturing" part of this exercise. My kids enjoy painting nails, "doing" hair, giving back massages, and rubbing lotion onto hands and feet as part of their home spa/beauty salon game. My job, as their #1 Customer, is to relax, enjoy, and try not to drool on my daughter's bedspread when I lie there half asleep during spa sessions.

Living an uncluttered life could be worse!

CHAPTER 4

THE TOY LESSON

It was a "Keeping Up With The Jones" kind of toy, but it turned into an important parenting opportunity for me.

The other girls at school had them – little plastic trolls, about one and a half inches high, with wild hair and potbellies. Who knows why they were the "in" thing, or why these ten-year-olds, who had almost outgrown dolls, were having such fun with them. I wondered if these were the new toy craze.

My daughter played with these girls at recess. She thought she had some of these trolls under her bed, so she promised she would bring them to school the next day. They weren't there. (I suspected we had donated them months ago. Ooops.)

She asked me if we could shop for some. I don't usually support requests like this, but it wasn't really a big deal. I thought it would be a nice thing to do for her. Homework needed to be done, so I promised to do some phone shopping if she'd get started.

I soon found some trolls so I called her dad and asked him to swing by the store on his way home. My daughter was excited when he brought in the troll. She couldn't get it out of the box. With the shrink wrap, plastic tape, staples, and stitching to keep the troll's hair in place, the packaging had probably cost more than the troll. Maybe this should have been a clue about the nature of this toy.

My daughter named the troll Mrs Green. Mrs Green had yellow hair and a green outfit. Mrs Green was about five inches tall. She was taller than the trolls at school, and my daughter thought that meant her troll could be "the mom." She was excited.

Later in the evening, after she had been in bed for a while, my daughter came into our room with tears in her eyes. She wanted to talk. It turns out that Mrs Green was too tall. It wasn't what she wanted. She had been lying in bed thinking about it and getting upset. Once it was out of the packaging and too late to return, she realized she wasn't happy with it.

Would I blow a "teaching" moment? I took a deep breath and asked her what she thought the solution might be. She said she didn't know and started to cry harder. So much for that parenting book. We were on our own.

I told her that Mrs Green was just "stuff." I told her what she felt is often the problem with "things." We sometimes give things the power to get under our skin and upset us when they really shouldn't. Things aren't people. No one was sick or dying. It was just a "thing" that had disappointed her.

I said many things eventually disappoint. Most "things" get worn out, lost, dated, broken or dirty. They are just "stuff." I said that what mattered was that her mom and dad loved her and wanted to help her by getting the troll.

I told her to enjoy Mrs Green. If the other kids teased her about the troll's size, I told her to put it away.

I told her we would keep our eyes peeled for smaller trolls, but it might be a while before we found one.

My daughter smiled and asked if stuff like this had ever bothered me when I was little. I said yes. I recalled an acrobatic doll that wasn't cuddly and I still think about a favorite childhood bracelet lost forever on an airplane trip.

Who hasn't had a toy disappoint them? She asked if I talked to my parents about stuff. I said yes. I could always go to my parents and talk to them about anything. I told her she could always talk to her dad or me about anything.

She gave me a hug and went back to bed. Whew! I hadn't blown it by being inattentive or impatient. Instead, I shared our family values about "stuff" with her. I had helped restore her perspective. Maybe Mrs Green will help me do better at keeping my own perspective the next time I lose an ear ring, break a camera, or don't find what I want at the mall.

CHAPTER 5

THE HUB OF THE HOME: REDUCE KITCHEN CLUTTER

The kitchen is the hub of our home, but I still struggle with how to maximize and best utilize this important family place. Sometimes it seems like everyone and everything passes through our kitchen. Here are a few general thoughts.

First, I have resolved to use my kitchen more often. Cook food in it. I am trying to spend time in it, rather than just toss my stuff, stand and eat a bowl of cereal, or pass through it.

Judging by the crowded restaurants I drive by, I am not alone here. Fast food really isn't faster or easier once I have to get in my car, drive there, park, and then wait. Interestingly enough, I have observed my kitchen stays cleaner when it is cooked in regularly. Counters and table get regularly wiped down this way.

Second, I am learning to be a minimalist in the kitchen. This begins with less clutter. When I have weeded out my kitchen, I am amazed by all the non-kitchen items that have worked their way onto my counters and into my precious kitchen cupboard space. Who would have known that kitchen cupboards would seem large and tempting compared to the small closets and other storage areas in my house? Or maybe non-kitchen stuff winds up in the kitchen cupboards because that's where someone is standing when they are seized by a desire to actually put something away? Put those things where they really belong! You will be able to find them then too!

Third, cut back on kitchen gadgetry. Have you noticed there is often something new to buy that you didn't realize you had to have until you saw the advertisement? (Think about rice cookers, sandwich makers, bread machines...) After you buy these must-have items, do you really keep using them? Try storing seasonal and infrequently used items in a large plastic tub or box elsewhere in the house to free up space for your daily kitchen activities.

Fourth, do you sometimes buy food you don't use? Maybe you had a coupon, or it was on sale, or you bought an ingredient for a recipe you wound up never making?

Sometimes I can't figure out why I have to go to the grocery store when my pantry and refrigerator already seem full. To clean out, I sometimes hold off buying groceries and make it a game to cook as many meals as I can with the food already at hand. Try cooking with fewer ingredients. I am learning not to quit on a recipe just because I am missing a couple of things. Who else will know something is missing if it is a stew, soup, or hot dish? Slowly, I learn to try making substitutions.

Finally, think functional rather than fanciful. My kitchen is easier to clean when I satisfy most of my knick-knack decorating urges elsewhere. I decided the tools I regularly cook with have their own utilitarian sort of beauty. Hang a broom on a bracket on the wall if you don't have a nearby closet. Add towel hooks for dishtowels and mount a paper towel holder under an upper cabinet if you want one handy. Worry less about looks. Your kitchen will look fine if it is clean and functional.

For more information on kitchen organization, check out the following websites. If you want help from a professional, www.napo.net lists their members, including a section with people who specialize in kitchen organizing.

Try www.thefamilycorner.com for numerous on-line articles on kitchen organizing that range from the fridge, to the pantry, to kitchen gadgets.

Finally, www.123sortit.com offers a detailed "recipe" for organizing your kitchen step by step.

Make your kitchen time special. Slow down to cook. Turn on

some music. Light a candle. One evening one of my daughters wondered out loud why I had lit a candle at the kitchen table before a weeknight dinner. My husband didn't miss a beat. He said, "If family isn't special enough to light a candle for, who is?"

CHAPTER 6

DON'T "KILL" CELERY AGAIN – CLEAR REFRIGERATOR CLUTTER

Has anyone else killed celery? You know what I mean. You buy a bunch of celery and use two stalks as called for in a recipe, and then you let the rest of it die a slow unnoticed death in the refrigerator. Does this sound familiar?

After a recent discussion on kitchen organization, some friends shared their refrigerator woes with me. Today I offer a few simple tips for organizing the refrigerator so that we rarely kill celery (or anything else) again.

Before anyone can simplify their refrigerator, they need to get rid of the dead and dying food there. Toss the obvious spoils – the stuff that looks bad, smells bad, or that you know is too old to eat. The next layer gets more interesting – this is the stuff you've pulled out in the past few months and said to yourself, "humm, not sure how old this is... better not chance it with a stomach ache today..."

After shaking your head, you carefully put these items back in the refrigerator. Will this food be safer to eat next week? No!

While you are at it, look in the refrigerator door too. "Finely aged" condiments may have enhanced flavors. Some of these are remnants in jars needed for a specific recipe you made months or even years ago. Do you know how old they are? Do you know if they are still safe to use? No! This food isn't getting any fresher or safer as you stall the inevitable. Don't waste your money on poison identification stickers for questionable food. Toss this stuff today. Don't risk making you or anyone else in your family sick. Feel guilty and wasteful once as you promptly dispose of this stuff and rinse out the jars for recycling. Firmly resolve to use that kitchen marker to date all future leftovers, condiments and all.

When you have weeded out your refrigerator, you will find you have the space to organize it in a logical way for your family. The next step to simplifying the refrigerator is to organize it just like a pantry. After all, the refrigerator is simply a chilled pantry. Group things logically by function. You could put all the sauces on one door shelf and all salad dressings on another door shelf. Meats could go in one bin (Don't store raw and cooked meats together because of cross contamination bacteria concerns), and cheeses could go in another bin. Fruits and vegetables could have their own compartments too.

You could create a snack shelf for the kids and a "Do not eat – Reserved for cooking!" shelf for you. Maybe you can put all the leftovers on one shelf toward the front so you will remember to use them.

Next, handle refrigerator food so you won't kill celery or anything else again. When I buy a bunch of celery and only use a couple of stalks, I chop the rest of it up anyway. I put it in half cup portions in sandwich bags. I nest these bags inside proper freezer bags, date them, and keep them in the freezer until needed for the next dish or until they get too old. This same principle also works for some of the other produce. Check your cookbook to see what should be cooked before frozen for safety or texture concerns.

Purge questionable refrigerator food, logically organize the refrigerator, freeze leftover produce, and menu plan to simplify the refrigerator.

Another tip to avoid refrigerator food waste is one you already know: Create a weekly menu plan and then shop weekly based on the plan. Most of us know we "should" do this. Very few of us take the time to do it. Busy lives, diverse activities for everyone in the family, and hectic schedules make this difficult.

That said, menu planning can be worth the effort and here is my strategy. Plan a menu based on three things: what needs to be used up in your refrigerator, what is on sale in the supermarkets, and what you haven't eaten for a while. Try keeping a simple dated list on the inside of a cupboard door of what you feed your family for the next month. This will help you menu plan.

If I can't persuade you to menu plan all the time, here is a back-up plan (often reality for many of us during busy weeks): Follow the 8am rule. Decide by 8am, or whatever time just before you leave the house every day, what is for dinner that night. Peek in the refrigerator. Take anything out of the freezer that needs to thaw in the refrigerator. Stop on your way home, if needed, to get any missing ingredients.

I like this back-up plan. I can't decide what to eat when I am tired and hungry at the end of the day. At that point, I am backed into a corner and I don't have a lot of choices. I can make a better decision in the morning when I am not worn out and hungry and I still have time to get any missing ingredients for dinner.

Keep the refrigerator organized by purging its contents weekly the evening before garbage day. If you can also make garbage day your shopping day, this will be even better because you will discover what you need to buy while you are cleaning out the refrigerator each week.

Besides, if my refrigerator is in better shape, I don't have to stand in front of its open door as long. This makes me less of a hypocrite when I yell at other family members for lingering in front of the open refrigerator door. Hey, if it is simpler, maybe we can all get in and out of the refrigerator faster too!

CHAPTER 7

KITCHEN ORGANIZING—GET OUT OF THE KITCHEN AND OUTSIDE!

Summer! I don't know about you, but I would rather be anywhere but stuck in my hot kitchen this time of year. I will share a few quick and easy kitchen-organizing tips to help minimize your time in the kitchen this summer. Here are a few questions to get you thinking.

Would you ever organize your spices in alphabetical order? I never thought I would. I tried to be organized, but alphabetizing spices still struck me as going too far. Then it happened. One winter I got tired of reading all the organizing "experts" who kept saying to alphabetize those spices. It was a long night. I was bored. I decided to try it out.

My spices had been on a shelf in our food closet. The ones I used most often were toward the front. Wasn't that logical enough? As I pulled everything out, I had a few surprises. Oops. I found several duplicates, numerous dried up globs in the bottoms of very old jars, and five jars, count them, five, of something called Five Spice Powder, used for stir fry. Five Spice Powder costs about $5 per jar. I wanted $20 back! What a waste. But now I was converted.

My spices are now alphabetized and on wire coated racks attached to the inside of my food closet door. To all of you who still aren't convinced, let me continue: putting your spice jars in alphabetical order prevents duplicate purchases. It speeds up menu planning because you can tell faster if you have what you need to make the recipe or not. It helps you generate a shopping list faster. You can even cook faster because you won't waste time hunting for assorted seasonings. Ultimately, you get out of the kitchen faster.

Do you date your spices? I am working on this one. I have heard that spices can last as little as six months or as long as two to three years. I am not ready to throw everything out and start over (though I have a friend who did this and she claims all her food suddenly tasted better). I do keep a permanent marker in my kitchen and I have started to date new spices as they come into my house. I also try to buy the smallest spice container available. A smaller container increases the chance that I will use it up before it gets too old.

Are your dry goods organized and stored simply? I am a big fan of rectangular, airtight, see-through containers. I got on this kick a few years ago. My husband had poured a bowl of cereal for himself from a previously opened box, and after several bites of cereal and milk, a small spider bubbled to the surface, scrambled to the edge of the bowl, and attempted to escape. Yum. Airtight containers keep food fresher (and spider-free).

Rectangular, or square containers make the best use of small spaces. No wasted corners. They will stack and fit next to each other well too.

See-through containers are great because certain members of my family, who shall remain anonymous, tend to put a nearly empty cereal or cracker box right back into the cupboard. This behavior foils my shopping attempts to keep our pantry stocked. I see what looks like a full box, but it really isn't. Surprise!

Organize food by type. Put all baking products on the same shelf. Group breakfast items together. Keep snack foods together. Keeping food categorized makes it faster for you to find and inventory what you have.

Are your kitchen cupboards crammed full of stuff? How many sets of dishes do you really need to store in the kitchen? You know the answer. How many coffee mugs would you ever really use all at once? Honestly, if more than six or eight people came to my house, I'd be getting out the disposables. So why was

I hanging on to all those mugs dating back to my high school days?

Do you have as many partial sets of unused stemware in your cupboard as I do? Consider keeping what you use and donating or storing the rest of it elsewhere.

As for cookbooks, I was finally able to reduce the excessive number when it dawned on me: How many recipes for apple crisp do I really need? Many cookbooks have a lot of similar recipes in common, plus I can find recipes on the Internet. There was a bonus too. Once I weeded out my cupboards, I actually had space for a few cookbooks in my kitchen.

How are those base cabinets? Does everything clatter out onto the floor when you try to make dinner? Base cabinets can be worse than uppers. Pots, pans, nesting bowls, and bakeware. Organize them to make meal preparation faster and easier. Keep only what you regularly use in these cabinets. Get rid of duplicates and extras. After all, how many sets of bowls do you really need?

Nest the pots and pans. Nest the lids and store them together too. I like using a wire lid rack to hold all my lids together from smallest to largest. Lid retrieval is now quieter too.

What kitchen clutter could you get rid of to make functioning in your kitchen easier? Here are some of my favorites to toss or to store elsewhere: extra plastic bags, plastic storage containers (especially if you can't find the matching lids), pots you don't use regularly, holiday platters and molds, assorted ceramic coffee mugs stacked deep in the cupboards, partial stemware sets you rarely use, duplicate utensils (three can openers? One is necessary but what do you need the other two for?), trendy or now dated appliances you haven't used in several years, burnt and scratched pots, pans, and bakeware that are too yucky to use any more – you know the ones I mean.

Last question: Do you have room to prepare food and a place to put it when you are ready to eat? When I manage to keep the kitchen counter free for making meals and to keep the kitchen table open for setting the table, my whole family gets in and out of the kitchen a lot faster.

We have a family rule about not setting stuff on the kitchen table, and I only keep what we use every day on the counter.

I hope these ideas are helpful.

I am out of here! See you at the beach!

Kitchen Organizing Catalogs and Websites

Though frugality is an important part of the simple living choices I make, I like to look at specialty stores for kitchen organizing and clutter control ideas. I don't necessarily purchase what I see, but it gets me thinking about other possible solutions. And sometimes, a specialty product is the best solution for a specific organizing situation. That said, you might want to check out the stores below:

- The Container Store at 1-888-266-8246 or www.container-store.com has many kitchen storage products. You may request a catalog.
- Get Organized at 1-800-803-9400 or www.shopgetorganized.com has organizing products in their catalog including some interesting specialty ones for the kitchen.
- www.kitchen101.com has kitchen utensils, gadgets, appliances, and links to 101 other kitchen sites
- www.organize.com is a site to check out lots of organizing products including a whole section devoted to kitchen items.

CHAPTER 8

WHAT IS A CLUTTER BUDDY?

I have not swapped clutter help with another person, but I plan to try it. I am inspired by a great experience I heard about from two people who tried it. Swapping clutter help is less expensive than hiring a professional organizer and possibly, more fun!

"Let's start at your house first," No, that's okay, let's start at your place." After getting over a little initial fear and embarrassment, the clutter buddies I spoke to reported that working with a partner to get rid of clutter made the job a lot more fun. Because someone was with them, it was easier to get down to the task in hand, and maintain a sense of humor throughout the clutter clearing tasks.

They also said there really weren't any rules. They dealt with everything from moving furniture, flipping mattresses, sorting papers, and weeding out junk mail and magazines. They didn't perform exactly the same tasks at each other's home, but they made a similar time commitment to each home.

The clutter buddies found that working with someone kept them on task for a longer time than a person can usually sort clutter on her own. Does anyone else besides me get tired, stiff, and lonely after a couple of hours hunched over paper piles on the floor?

Getting help from a buddy also eliminated guilt. This wasn't wasting someone else's time. It was an even exchange of time and effort. The clutter buddies reported it was easier to work on someone else's clutter rather than their own. They didn't have an emotional investment in each other's stuff, so they were able to help each other objectively. What a gift!

The clutter buddies also made it fun. They took breaks and rewarded themselves.

At one home, they shared homemade soup, and at another soon-to-be-clutter-free person's house, they went out to eat before coming back to finish up. All in all, they spent over 12 hours at each home. Two people working together for 12 hours is 24 hours of clutter control. That is a lot longer than my usual hour or two at home alone. The clutter buddies got a lot done!

Finally, the buddies I spoke to said since it worked so well the first time, they got together again and they have already scheduled a third time on their calendars.

CHAPTER 9

HOUSEHOLD CHAOS: REAL OR PERCEIVED?

Do you suffer from CHAOS – Can't Have Anybody Over Syndrome (a term from Marla Cilley, the FlyLady)? Does your clutter or housekeeping prevent you from entertaining? Are you afraid to have people over because of what they might think of you when they see your home?

You know you aren't alone. Right?

CHAOS is a term I learned at the clutter control website: www.flylady.net from Marla Cilley who is also the author of a book called *Sink Reflections*.

I don't rave about many websites. The FlyLady's website is different. I find her site to be full of house cleaning and organizing tips. And what's more, it is humorous and motivational. I especially enjoy the free cheerful daily email reminders that you can sign up for to motivate you and to help you stay on track. The FlyLady takes you through every step of the way, every day, as you form many new small habits to clean and organize your home. She calls them baby steps.

I would like to suggest that CHAOS comes in two forms — real and perceived.

Real CHAOS is physical. It is the kind you trip over or see stacked up in piles on every available surface. FlyLady's website can help with that.

Perceived CHAOS, though, is a mental state that comes from living in modern America.

I worry about perceived CHAOS.

"We can't have anyone over until the new furniture comes."

"I'll invite you over after we get the deck built."

"We'll try to get together later this summer after we get the landscaping whipped into shape." "My house has exploded. I can't have you over until I put it back together."

I have heard comments like this from many people.

Here are other comments that may not be said out loud but contribute to this perceived CHAOS: "If I buy this, my house will be more acceptable."

"I need to run to the mall and get this before our company comes over this weekend."

"I'll get the house cleaned and then it will be okay if they come over."

Wow, we certainly have succumbed to marketing and consumerism if we let these thoughts impair our opportunities to socialize.

On top of that, the "in" stuff to own changes by the season and by the year. "Eeeeew, those are last year's hip margarita glasses. Don't you have the new ones?" Hooray for marketing. They've thrown us a line, and we keep buying it (literally) — hook, line and sinker.

If I shop 'til I drop, will I have acquired enough of the "right stuff" to be able to entertain people in my home? Do I have to create the right "look" in my home before I can invite my friends over? Does my house have to be perfectly clean before I can invite other people in? Many of us have gotten this societal message that we have to own the right things and have them properly cleaned and organized before we can invite people into our home.

If you think about it, isn't that sad? I think less entertaining happens now than twenty years ago because of this perception, this perceived CHAOS. Do you really care if someone's house is perfect when you are invited over, or are you just happy to get the invitation?

I am really more comfortable with people in homes that aren't perfect but the people are relaxed about their home and just happy to see me. Since they are relaxed and their house is relaxed, I can be relaxed there too.

When I invite people over, I am asking them to come spend time with me. I am not asking them to take a bath in my not-perfectly-scrubbed-out bathtub or to look for dust bunnies under my furniture. Yet, many of us hesitate to get together with each other if things aren't "perfect."

Maybe we just need to get over it. Isn't it more important to stay connected with people rather than to entertain in a perfect home? Practice. Try inviting someone over and not cleaning your house. Try it again a week later with another friend... and again .... You get the idea.

By the way, the "Fly" in "FlyLady" stands for "Finally Loving Yourself," a term coined by one of her appreciative fans. Maybe that is what it really is about: We have to love ourselves enough to trust that others will too, whether our home is "perfect" or not.

CHAPTER 10

A SIMPLE FAMILY VACATION —NOT SO SIMPLE

Hypocrite. That's me. Our simple vacation one summer was anything but simple. We rented several cabins with my in-laws, as we have done every year. It was supposed to be a week of quiet fishing up north. It really wasn't that simple.

We have to bring everything. I mean everything. We pack clothes for all weather, toiletries, kitchen supplies, towels, boat, stuff for boat, stuff for kids, stuff for swimming, stuff for fishing, stuff for kids...

My *clutter-free* list of stuff to pack is over four pages long.

Our vacation does not include many life-simplifying amenities. A drive in to town is a major trip. There are few modern conveniences. There are no televisions, dishwashers, or laundering facilities, and no phones (cell phones are out of range).

Our simple vacations are not always uneventful. One year all our vehicles, including the boat, had hail damage during a quick storm that blew in off the lake the day we arrived. There was also a field mouse in Grandma's cabin. One year it was so hot for several days and nights, that no one could sleep or do anything. One year cloudy, rainy, and cold weather all week challenged our ability to entertain the kids. Another year, a hidden stump damaged the lower unit of our boat as we crossed the lake. One year, a skunk heavily doused one of our dogs. We had no supplies to deal with it. Every year we graciously serve as a smorgasbord for numerous mosquitoes inside and outside the cabins.

On top of that, we sometimes are too busy on vacation. We try to pack in sight seeing, personal time for napping and reading, trips into town, family time for playing games and visiting, and several large meals together every day. We also cram fishing, swimming, and boating into one short week.

How dare I share my thoughts on a reduced clutter vacation? I shouldn't. That said, here are the "pearls of wisdom" from the dark side of my experiences.

Lists

Keep "vacation to-do lists" from year to year. Mail, newspapers, phone, pet care, and securing the house must be dealt with every vacation. I don't have time to reinvent this list two weeks before we leave every year.

Keep packing lists from year to year. My friend Mary does this on her computer, and I learned this is helpful too. I also finally learned to put the pet sitter's instructions on computer. Now I don't have to look up the phone number of our vet and the address and phone for the resort every year. Besides, the pet sitters couldn't read my handwriting any way!

Update packing lists right after you get home. There are usually a few things I wish I had brought, and there are a few things I brought that I didn't need to bring. If I don't update my lists, I forget about those items by next year. Even with lists, I still bring too much food. Yet, I can revise my lists yearly, so we learn from our previous experiences.

Time Management

Don't overbook your time. Busy. Busy. Busy. That's too busy when we're trying to relax. We sometimes try to cram too much into our vacations. We go fishing in the early morning. We go on adventures or swim or boat in the afternoon, and we stay up late building fires, playing cards, and socializing. I also bring too many books to read and I carry too many fantasies in my head about personal time for myself.

We work hard during the year, and sometimes we try to play too hard on vacation. Maybe the trick, if there is one, is to pick one or two vacation goals and stick with them.

A vacation could be a personal retreat, or a time to spend with family, a time to fish, or an area to explore and go sight seeing. Six days can't accomplish an unrealistic number of goals. I think it can be frustrating to have a short multi-purpose vacation.

What is a vacation "supposed to" accomplish, if anything? For me, a vacation is a break from my regular routine. When we go up north to the cabins, it certainly isn't a break from cooking and household activities! It is time fishing with my kids and beautiful scenery to enjoy. Maybe I need to go to a spa or take a personal retreat if I want to accomplish the other (fantasy) goals in my head.

Ten Days to Two Weeks

My last suggestion would be to stay for longer than a week if you can. In our fast-paced society, I think it may take many of us longer than one short week to really wind down. Maybe a longer break from the routine would be in order. If I still insist on overbooking my vacation, at least I could accomplish more in two weeks than I can in one.

Final Thought: A personal retreat — this tired mom's idea for a personal break

I love my family. I really do. But (could you tell there was a "but" coming?) I finally realized I am a better worker, spouse, parent... if I take some time once in a while just for me.

Besides the usual dinners or movies out with friends, this means I take personal retreats.

The Woman's Retreat Book by Jennifer Louden is a great place to start for retreat ideas. She offers many ideas for different types of retreats and different lengths of retreats.

We are also lucky to live where we do. Our metro area has

many retreat centers that offer individual as well as group retreats, and even family reunion retreats. Many of them have nice scenery. Most include meals. Someone else gets to cook and clean up!

For retreat options in your area, just check the phone book's yellow page listing under "Retreat Facilities." You may be surprised by the options you find.

Retreat centers tend to be more reasonably priced than hotels especially since they often include meals. If you are looking for rest, reading, connecting with nature, or personal reflection, they are something to consider. Many offer walking areas, and perhaps a pool or sauna or even a therapeutic massage. If you are looking for television, telephones, and shopping, look elsewhere!

CHAPTER 11

HAPPY 4TH OF JULY: UNCLUTTER YOUR PERSONAL HISTORICAL TREASURES

The 4th of July isn't just about picnics, parades, and fireworks. It is a celebration of our American heritage. It is easy for me to forget that. I get caught up in the fun activities. It is easy to live in the holiday moment. I am trying to get better at putting this holiday into historical perspective, not just for me, but also for my children.

On the topic of history, I had a glimpse of personal historical perspective: my childhood bedroom finally got cleaned out.

During a visit, I was sent home with the bittersweet remains — the cracked blue Mason jar filled with marbles, the high school bowling trophies, and several boxes of clothing and parapher-nalia dating back to the 1970's.

Common sense said it might be best to just toss this clutter memorabilia. After all, I had managed to get along just fine without this stuff for almost 20 years. I just didn't have the space or energy to keep storing it all. I had selfishly liked the fact that it still existed and that my parents had taken care of it for me all this time. But it really wasn't fair to them or responsible of me. Now that they had lightened up and cleaned it out, what was I supposed to do? Toss it all? How could I preserve the memories without resorting to stacking boxes in my basement or paying for off-site storage?

I decided to follow my own advice. Armed with my journal, my camera, and a couple of hours when I felt rested and rational, I approached the boxes that were stacked downstairs temporarily. As I explored their contents, I observed that the stuff there pretty much fell into three categories: memories, donations, and keepers.

As I began to sort, the question was: trash or treasure from my past?

Memories. It was fun to look at the old clothes — the one and only shirt I had ever tried to sew back in 7th grade home economics class, the scarf shirt my mom made for me so I could be 1980's "cool", the faded marching band shirts. Some of this stuff couldn't be saved. It was too dated and worn to be any use to anyone. Perhaps some of it would make cleaning rags. It was fun to look at, and I didn't want to forget what I had seen. I began to list some of these things, describe them, and talk about them in my personal journal. I could preserve their memory without storing the items themselves.

Donations. Some of the stuff in the boxes was good enough to donate. Some of the clothing was in good shape and neutral enough to survive the test of time. If it also represented a special memory for me, I wrote in my journal about it, and then I added it to the growing donation pile on the floor. I had to repeatedly remind myself that I had plenty and that it was important to send this stuff on to help others while it still had some functional life left.

Some things, like the old hats, were just too bulky to keep. Other things were very specific to me (trophies even had my name on them), so I lined them up and took a few photographs to go with my journal entries. Photographing stuff that is bulky to store is another way to preserve the memory without storing the clutter. But... not everything was clutter either.

Keepers. For lack of space and to keep it simple, I wanted to be picky about what I kept. Some items were still too special for me to toss or to donate. There were some things, like the marbles, that I thought my daughters would have a little fun with now or in the not-too-distant future. In the end, I wound up with a few things I gave to my girls right away and a few things that fit into just one box.

Reliving childhood memories and making decisions wasn't simple or easy, but it was gratifying and important to stay connected with my own personal heritage. These are personal choices. Keep what is beautiful, useful, and sentimental to you. After all, clearing clutter is not about tossing it all.

CHAPTER 12

THE PAPER AIRPLANE: CHILDREN'S TRASH OR TREASURE?

Every day I am faced with many decisions about what treasures to keep and what to toss. How do I decide? How does anyone? How can I hang onto the feelings and details of the moment without creating boxes and boxes of memorabilia?

"You can't come in here. Wait, Mom! Don't peek!" My kids run into the hallway and slam the door. I stand, puzzled, in my youngest daughter's bedroom. What are they up to now?

Automatically, I start to straighten things up in the bedroom as I stand there. I sense motion and when I look down, there it is. A paper airplane is lying at my feet. On the top of it, it says, "Dear Mom, open me up." It is taped. I carefully peel the tape off the underside of the paper airplane. Underneath, hidden in the folds, they have written, "I love You Mom." Below that are three concentric hearts and inside them in smaller print, it says, "I Love You."

I smile. I track down my daughters to hug them and thank them. Now what do I do? Crumple up this treasure and toss it in the wastebasket? Save it for posterity? It didn't take a lot of effort for them to make it, but I appreciated the fun and sentiment that went into it.

It isn't just the paper airplane. Last week it was the doctor kit — a white plastic case filled with toy doctoring items, some in pretty bad shape from heavy usage. I found it in the family playroom. It hadn't been played with for months. I ask my daughters, "So, are you guys still using this?" The answers come back, "Not really," and "Well, maybe sometimes…"

What am I supposed to do now? I can't save everything.

Sometimes I want to. It feels like time slips through my fingers like water. The more I try to hang onto it, the faster it dribbles away.

Sometimes I hope that hanging onto stuff, or making video-tapes, or taking numerous photos will capture the moment. But really it won't.

Preserving this stuff creates clutter and causes me to lose the chance to live these moments as I busily struggle to capture them. Think about it: Are you the person in front of the camera experiencing the moment or are you the one often standing behind the camera trying to capture the moment?

What is the solution? The answer probably varies for each of us, as we struggle to simplify our lives, still preserve family history, and live the moment. Part of the answer for me is writing in a journal. After all, it is the thoughts and feelings I want to share and preserve, not the stuff.

Don't get hung up on the "should's" or "ought to's" of keeping a journal. Here are some thoughts I'd like to share:

Journaling. Write as often or as infrequently as you want to write. Don't write regularly because you feel you "should" or because you are "supposed to" do it every day.

My early childhood diaries all had dated page numbers in them. If I missed for a while, I felt so bad about the blank pages that I usually wound up abandoning the whole diary.

Write about what you want to write about and what you feel rather than about details you think you "should" record for posterity. Which is more interesting? "It is a sunny day and I took you to the park and pushed you on the swing," or "As I pushed you on the swing in the park today, I felt guilty for feeling a little bored." I think honest thoughts make insightful and interesting observations to include.

Write about childhood treasures that you choose not to save. Think about what will happen when someone else, probably one of your children, cleans out your clutter in 30 years. Which would be more interesting to them – a crumpled paper airplane or a journal entry describing the paper airplane and explaining what happened that day?

Writing helps unclutter my closets and my mind. It leaves a record that my kids may someday appreciate. Maybe they will even identify with some of my thoughts if they ever have kids of their own. As a bonus, writing helps me work through daily life stuff. When it gets right down to it, we are all just renters and borrowers in the material world. If I write, maybe I can preserve the ideas and feelings for posterity instead of the stuff.

CHAPTER 13

SLOW DOWN SUMMER!

Does summer speed along too fast? Do you feel hectic and hurried rather than rested and relaxed? I look forward to summer, but it seems like it slips by more quickly every year. Vacations, swimming lessons, activities for the kids, social events, and yard and home improvement projects make summer way too rushed.

Life is anything but simple, even in the summer. Maybe especially in the summer. So much to do and so little time. My family and I hurry from one activity to the next, sometimes barely taking time to appreciate them. Sometimes the stuff that is supposed to be fun doesn't feel fun because we are so busy. Hectic schedules eat away at what is supposed to be a summer *break*.

Here are tips to simplify summer time and enjoy the remainder of the summer at a simpler pace. There are ways to change your time perception and techniques to appreciate these wonderful summer days. Time management tricks to handle time efficiently are covered in Summer Section chapter 15 and chapter 16, and Fall Section, chapter 1 and chapter 2.

Do you hurry time along? I suggest a simple exercise for you to check your own pace. It sounds corny, but if you try it, you may be surprised by the results.

Ask a friend or family member to time you with a watch, or use a stop watch or kitchen timer by yourself. Begin by sitting quietly and closing your eyes. Do nothing but sit and relax. See if you can set your internal clock for three minutes (no fair counting!). Open your eyes and check the time when you think three minutes has elapsed. How did you do?

For many of us, three minutes sitting quietly with our eyes closed will seem like an eternity. We will speed things up and feel that three minutes elapsed well before three minutes of real time passed. Maybe we are used to living lives that are too "speeded up."

To slow down to a more enjoyable pace, regularly do more activities that you "lose yourself" in. These are activities so engrossing to you personally that you get pulled into the flow and you don't realize how much time has passed. You will know what these things are if you take a few moments to think about it. Some people like to read. Others like to sew or work on a favorite project or hobby. Still others might exercise or bike. It could be anything. Everyone is unique.

Time won't necessarily slow down when you do these things. In fact, favorites often make time fly for people. But, it flies by in an enjoyable way that leaves you energized, centered, and refreshed. When you allow yourself to do your personal favorites, you find yourself thinking afterwards, "Wow, I really liked that. I forgot how much I enjoy doing that. I could do that more often." After thinking that, many of us go directly back to the other hectic demands in our lives. Stop. Give yourself permission to do the things you love. Give permission more often.

Find activities that stretch time for you. For many, quiet nature walks or sitting and looking at a lake can slow things down and stretch out time. Getting out and enjoying nature also provides perspective and balance in harried lives. Spending time outside can literally help us spend time outside of ourselves and our worries and problems. Time outside of ourselves can give us perspective in our lives.

Would you consider trying meditation for a change of pace? Meditation isn't just for the "experts." There are many simple forms of meditation. A classic that provides several easy ways to begin to meditate is *How to Meditate* by Lawrence LeShan. You can take as little as ten minutes to meditate if you want. Meditation can be a tool to slow down and refocus. It isn't as hard to do as you may think it is!

If meditating isn't your cup of tea, consider taking five minutes to half an hour to do nothing. Yes, I mean nothing. I don't mean watching television, doing a routine task, or even starting to mentally compose your to-do list. Taking time to do nothing will slow you down. It may even make you fidgety. Doing nothing for a short while will prepare you to plunge in with new energy for whatever tasks or summer pleasures are waiting for you.

Try to live in the moment. Focus totally on doing one thing at a time. I know we are all supposed to multi-task, and sometimes we must. Unfortunately, multi-tasking often leaves us stressed and unfocused. We feel fragmented and splintered.

Focusing on one thing at a time helps us to be really present instead of preoccupied. When I am with my kids, I know they can tell if I am really present, or if I am multi-tasking. It's a "no brainer" to guess which version of Mom they prefer.

Slow down. If I can't get it all done today anyway, maybe I can sometimes ease up to be a little kinder to myself. I know that when I slow down, I enjoy myself more. I think I am easier on the people around me, and I am probably more fun to be around.

Are you saying, "I don't have time?" Try to make time for yourself. Unfortunately, no one else can do this for you. Remember, how you spend the rest of this summer is your choice. Make choices that work for you.

Helpful Time Stretching Time Management Books

The three books below present an interesting perspective of our harried society and provide practical tips to improve the quality of your time. Rather than being time management books in the traditional sense, they offer suggestions to change how you perceive and utilize your time.

Time Shifting – Creating More Time to Enjoy your Life by Stephan Rechtschaffen.

Slowing Down in a Speeded Up World by Adair Lara.

Taking Your Time – Finding Balance in a Hurried World by Eknath Easwaran.

CHAPTER 14

THE SWIMMING LESSON: QUALITY TIME OR QUANTITY TIME?

It was a hot sticky day at the indoor pool in our local YMCA. The air was so hot and humid it was difficult to breathe. The noise from the kids in the pool was a dull roar reverberating in an echo chamber. Parents perched uncomfortably on sticky little plastic stools scattered around the perimeter of the pool. I regretted not bringing a book or a magazine. I wanted to be a "bad mom" and walk away from my daughters' swimming lessons to step outside where at least there was a breeze or go hide in an air-conditioned spot. I don't know why I stuck it out. Maybe I was already too drowsy from the heat to bother to move.

But wait! What happened? My eldest just shot from one end of the pool to the other. Finally, she was rolling her head to breathe and actually making forward progress with her front crawl! I saw the "high fives" she exchanged with her teacher. Next, she sought out *my* eyes. I jumped to my feet and gave her my enthusiastic thumbs up. As I sheepishly sat back down, I realized I had almost missed it: a moment of triumph. If I had left or even mentally faded off, I would have missed that moment in her life.

It is inevitable that I will miss many important moments, but I have learned the hard way that I can't often create special moments or quality time in my family's life. All I can do is simply try to be there for as many of those moments as I can. Though time efficiency experts urge us to cram as much into every day as we can, I want to share three other techniques to appreciate time and help summer from slipping away:

Don't always multi-task. What? Surely, I could get more done if

I caught up on my reading *and* took the kids to their swimming class! But, if my eyes had been down in a book, I would have missed my daughter's moment of triumph. Quality time means not doing two or three things at once. I am still learning this. Sometimes I try to multi-task while interacting with my kids. I am only fooling myself if I think they don't know they don't really have my full attention. How do I feel when I know someone isn't really listening to me? When I put multi-tasking on hold, at least some of the time, I am rewarded.

Log as much quantity time as possible to find quality time. I would really like to fool myself here. Yes, a mom can create quality time for her family. However, I am tired of dragging my kids to all the carnivals in the area for "special family moments". Will I be a bad mom if my kids have only had their youthful faces painted half a dozen times instead of 30? What is really a quality moment? Is it only to be found in face painting or junk food? Some of the time when I try to orchestrate quality family time, it turns into a phony hassle. Instead, I think I just have to do my time, as much time as I can around work, home chores, and life in general. Like at the pool. If I hadn't been sitting there at each lesson, I would have missed the brief moment of my daughter's swimming success.

Cut back on activities. This is the hardest one. I don't like to admit I can't do it all. In fact, it isn't even fun any more to try to do it all. Make the tough choices on what you devote your time to and don't second-guess yourself. We didn't have to be at swimming that day. We had a dozen other activities we could have done instead. In our boating and fishing life, however, water safety is a priority. We needed to be at swimming lessons. If I sign my kids up for swimming, tennis, softball, soccer... there is no quality time, only running around. The less I overbook, the more my family is rewarded. Frankly, I am pleased to see that my kids have started to learn how to creatively entertain themselves when we have a break in the action. I think that is a useful life skill.

For my personal sanity and for the sake of a slower and more satisfactory summer, I try to do one thing at a time, focus on each activity, and make the tough choices to cut back on activities.

It isn't easy. Some days, like a kid in a candy store — distracted by all the opportunities I see, I can't focus on any one thing, and I want it all. I am happier, though, when I make my choice, stay focused, and stay in the moment to enjoy it. I can choose to spend as much time as I can with my children to find the quality moments.

CHAPTER 15

CLEAR HECTIC FALL SCHEDULE CLUTTER NOW

The fallacy of summer, especially in the Midwest, is how we look forward to it, and then, when it is here, we wish it away. You would think we would learn. In winter, trapped inside our homes and sick of piling on layers of clothing to go outside to shovel snow, we eagerly look forward to summer. Yet, in the dog days of summer, we hide in our air-conditioned homes and offices, complain about the heat index and the mosquitoes, and dread ducking out to cut the grass or weed the garden. I hear people wish the hot summer away and yearn for fall.

Listen to us! We fantasize about lazy summer days, but we overbook. We are honest enough to admit fall is busy, but are we happy about it? As we prepare to swap hectic summer schedules for even busier fall ones, I share the principles that help me simplify fall at our house: delegation, calendar management, and priorities.

Delegate fall preparations. Delegate. Delegate. Delegate. It is a mantra I repeat for my own benefit. I want things the way I want them. Having strong preferences puts me in charge of the show. That gets tiring. I slowly learn I am happier if I don't do it all. Not only is it better for me to delegate, it is better for other family members too.

This time I give the kids their own school supply lists and let them shop for themselves. I put them in charge of figuring out which clothing in their closets is outgrown. I suggest they make their own lists before they shop. They need to learn. I need to let go.

Try letting children manage their own music practice and homework this fall. Consider putting kids in charge of making their beds and handling their own morning routines. Assign a couple more chores for each child to teach them responsibility. I slowly learn I can't do it all, and I discover that I can get help if I am willing to delegate.

"Underbook" the family fall calendar. Take the time now to write in everyone's schedule, including games, practices, lessons, and meetings. Write in the things you already know to help prevent overbooking. Look hard at what is already there before you add more. How many nights per week do you really want to be on the go?

Try to leave open spots. Create room for you and your family to breathe and to relax. An uncluttered calendar is like an uncluttered closet or cupboard. It feels better. There is room to grow. There is potential! Overbooking is often a familiar pattern like the habit of tossing stuff into a closet with the mental promise to yourself that you will come back and organize it later. Right... Hold fast to your intentions and stay out of the same overbooked rut. Limit activities. Learn to enjoy free time, even in the fall.

Stay on track with your priorities. We had the summer off. Even if we have been too busy, we still had a break from the regular routine.

Right now it might be time to review those New Year's resolutions from months ago. It isn't too late to achieve them. Weight loss? It isn't too late to diet now, before the holidays. Planning to take a class this year? Work on a hobby? Clean out a closet? Check out your goals and then plan your fall to achieve them. It isn't too late to make progress.

To get a few more ideas for your new, improved fall schedule, check out the following books: *Time Management from the Inside Out: The Foolproof System for Taking Control of Your Schedule and*

Your Life, by Julie Morgenstern, *Raising Self-Reliant Children in a Self-Indulgent World: Seven Building Blocks for Developing Capable Young People*, by H. Stephen Glenn and Jane Ed.D. Nelson, and *Confessions of a Happily Organized Family* by Deniece Schofield.

If web surfing is more your style, try www.simpleliving.net or www.organizedhome.com for simple living and organizing ideas.

Use the last couple weeks of summer to regroup and rethink your fall strategy.

CHAPTER 16

ORGANIZE YOUR FALL TIME: GOAL SETTING

A few weeks before school starts, I start to get a knot in my stomach. I am not ready for fall. The kids aren't ready for fall. Where did summer go? How are we going to get everything done this fall? How can we keep from overbooking ourselves and feeling so rushed? I feel a queasy panic.

Can you relate to this? Many of us spend the last few weeks of summer commenting about how busy our lives will get this fall. Activities and school start up again, and, good grief, even Christmas is coming! Life gets hectic. How can we be less busy, but still accomplish what we want? I will share a basic time management technique to help keep things under control. It can keep you and your family on track for fall or for life.

For me, the best step to manage time effectively and prevent becoming overwhelmed is to have a plan. The experts call it "goal setting."

It is simple. Set life goals, then five-year goals, and then one-year goals. After that, pull the one-year goals into monthly and then weekly, and finally daily to-do lists. I think of my to-do lists as the physical representation of where I want my life to go.

Yeah. Yeah. Yeah. We've all heard about goal setting. It feels a little like going to the dentist or buying life insurance. It is one of those things most of us agree we probably would be wise to do, someday, but we delay because it isn't "fun" or the rewards don't seem as tangible as a new purchase or a remodel.

Why is it important to set goals today? Because our time is our life! That's it. No commercials. You can't rewind your life tape when you get to the end.

Do you know anyone who spends more time and energy researching a new purchase, like an oven or television, than they spend planning their life? Think about that the next time you spend a day at the mall looking for something to make your life better. I say that because I have been there, at the mall, unconsciously trying to fix my life by purchasing just the right thing.

Now I have discovered if I set goals and work on them, I really can change my life. I believe this. Another funny thing is that planning or goal setting really doesn't take long. Less than a day at the mall. You could grab a piece of paper and be done in less than an hour.

Here is a manageable list of life areas to set goals:

- Family/Relationship
- Professional/Career
- Financial
- Personal/Self development
- Community Service
- Spiritual/Religious
- Social/Relaxation
- Health/Exercise

There. That wasn't so bad, was it? It was a reasonable number (8). You might even cross out or prioritize the goal areas. Put them in order of priority for you. You could also create other categories for yourself. Some of us might even include a "material stuff" or "travel" category, acknowledging that many of us look forward to and plan major purchases and vacations. Regardless of the categories we choose, most of us could spend five to ten minutes thinking about each area of our life and jotting down some life goals.

So what is the trick to make goal-setting really work?

Well, there are three tricks or techniques. First, we must break broad life goals down into practical action steps that eventually get incorporated into a daily to-do list. A broad goal such as "I want to spend the rest of my life being more physically fit" might become a one-year goal to "Lose thirty pounds." The monthly goal could be "Join a health club," and then the weekly goal would be to "Exercise on Monday, Wednesday, and Friday morning."

Effective goals are specific, measurable, and doable. If they aren't specific (lose 30 pounds), how do you decide when you reach your goal? If they aren't measurable (get on the scale), how can you track your progress? And, finally, if they aren't doable (lose 30 pounds in two weeks. Hah!), well, it won't be realistic for you to get it done.

A tip from those who are consistently better at achieving their goals than the rest of us: Recognize life's interruptions, and make contingency plans for your goals right away.

For example, plan that if you miss exercising once during the week, you will get up early on Saturday to do it. Contingency plan development on the front end is what separates the professional from the amateur goal setter.

Another tip I learned in Weight Watchers is this: Recommit. Recommit. Recommit. If you were on a diet and fell off the wagon last night, don't quit. Simply recommit. Recommit as many times per month, week, or even day as you need to get back on track and eventually achieve your desire!

The second technique is to save and periodically review your life goals to track your progress. It won't take long. Just jot it on your calendar quarterly. Pull out your original plan. Remind yourself of your priorities. See how you are doing. This will help you stay on course. You won't let important things slip away. You will be motivated to continue when you start to see your progress.

The third technique is to prioritize your daily to-do list, and do your high-priority stuff first. Your list for the day might be:

pick up milk, mow the yard, buy a birthday gift for Saturday, and exercise. Are all items equally important? Maybe you must pick up milk for your family. Maybe you want to mow the yard before it gets too long. You know you have to exercise—it is a priority, and so you admit you could get the birthday gift tomorrow.

When I make time to work on priority to-do items, I am happier. I feel satisfied because I make progress in life areas that really matter to me. How I spend my day or my week or my life is my choice. So, next time you get bogged down with fall busyness, consider goal setting to prioritize and simplify your life.

Goal Setting Resources & Books

To make the transition from life goals to daily to-do lists, consider buying or creating a personal planner. Check out office supply stores to find all sorts of planners and calendars. Don't be shy about creating your own categories and tailoring them to fit your life. Something will fit your style! Remember, though, there isn't a product out there that will manage your time or your life for you. You still get to do that part!

Here are a couple of time management books that provide goal-setting ideas:

How To Get Control of Your Time and Your Life by Alan Lakein is a classic time management book that many subsequent books are based on. Why not read the original? It focuses on goal setting.

The Overwhelmed Person's Guide to Time Management by Ronni Eisenberg with Kate Kelly covers goal setting and other helpful techniques to manage time more efficiently.

~

Section 4
Fall

~

CHAPTER 1

PRACTICAL TIME MANAGEMENT

"Dear Diary,
The kids are almost back in school. I must gear up for my fall business.

Summer draws to a close. Fatigue and change are in the air. The stress of upcoming holidays is an annoying buzz just under my daily consciousness.

Sometimes I wonder how other people do it. Do they have more hours in their day than I do? How can I plan ahead for fall and for the holidays and be prepared? After all, this stuff is seasonal! The calendar year repeats itself over and over again.

It seems like I could catch on faster, but instead I usually feel like someone chasing a merry-go-round that has started before I could quite climb on."

Simplify Your Week Nights

The days are still long – though not for much longer! We put a lot of pressure on our poor little summer. We are supposed to do all our usual stuff, plus yard work, outside projects and have some good old-fashioned fun in this tiny window of opportunity. Now school and other fall activities and routines begin.

I am guilty of trying to cram way too much into a 24-hour day. I struggle to accomplish as much as I can in the weekly Monday to Friday grind. During this busy week, I try to capture that elusive thing some people call "leisure time" or "family time" in this brief season of late summer or early fall. How can we get it all done, especially during the week?

Here are some ideas that help me in my quest for mid-week free time — that is, when I remember to use them:

Have week night schedules for errand running, household care and meals.

For example, maybe Wednesday is errand night, Thursday is laundry night, and Friday is pizza night. Try not to run errands on weekends because everyone else has the same bright idea. You will spend more time standing in line than getting things done.

Meals require less mental effort if you are willing to let them be scheduled too.

Somewhere along the line, we have gotten the idea that schedules and habits are restrictive things. I would like to suggest that schedules are actually very freeing. Try to put household tasks on a schedule. Why? So you don't have to worry about them or even think about them the other six days of the week!

Turn off the television on week nights.

Eliminate this time waster to free up time for things you need to get done and things you want to get done. Possible exception: Use television to entertain young children while you get dinner on the table. This isn't "cheating" if it saves your sanity and makes you a calmer parent. Right?

Take a walk around the block.

I actually have to remind myself to do this, so I am not totally embarrassed to include it. There is something about being outside, even for a short period on a hot muggy day, which unties mental knots like nothing else can. It also is a great chance to meet and to connect with neighbors. After all, if we are all going to hide inside with our air conditioners, it might as well be winter. If you don't believe me, I ask you to try it three times in the next week, before you tell me it was foolish to mention. Please.

Go to bed at the same time every night.

Give yourself at least 15 minutes of winding down time every night — something just for you such as reading time, a relaxing shower, or a conversation with a partner. Try using this time for anything you consider relaxing except watching television. Why not television? Come on! Who watches television for 15 minutes and then promptly turns it off? Don't get hooked and subsequently tired! We all need relaxation and rest. Our bodies appreciate a regular routine too.

Take time to plan and schedule leisure, fun, and family activities for the weekend.

If I don't make the effort to schedule the "good stuff" on the weekend calendar, it gets swallowed up by errands, projects, and even Saturday morning cartoons.

Do you ever ask yourself, "Where did the weekend go?" There will usually be an endless to-do list of things to go buy or household projects to tackle.

Take it upon yourself to make sure the fun stuff happens too. When I am at the mall, there is a little nagging voice in my head telling me that my time could be better spent elsewhere. Guess what? When I am on a family bike ride or reading with one of my kids, that yucky little voice is gone. It is up to me to schedule the right stuff.

Finally, get rid of the guilt. When will we learn that we really can't have our cake and eat it too? At least, we can't have it all in the same tiny window of time! From the time you walk in the door to the time you go to bed on a week night, you only have four or five hours to deal with dinner, children's sporting events, homework, errands, household tasks, the mail, and whatever you brought home from work.

Give yourself a break. After all, if you don't, who will?

CHAPTER 2

TIME MANAGEMENT TIPS
FOR FALL

On your marks. Get set. Go. Fall is here. Summer is over. Back to school and the usual busy routines. How can we manage it all any better? How can we simplify over-crowded schedules?

I hesitate to offer my suggestions because I am afraid, by themselves, these ideas won't help unclutter your life.

Warning! The time management or efficiency tips here will only take you so far. Our time is analogous to a small closet. There is a limited space to fill. I can use lots of clever storage techniques to improve the use of my small closet. But, once I have implemented them, the closet is full. If I keep dragging home more stuff to cram into the closet, I am going to be just as unhappy as I was before I organized it.

It is like that with time. We have a limited quantity – 24 hours per day. Skilled use of time efficiency tips can be like getting Superman or Superwoman powers. You can accomplish a lot. Or, you can run yourself ragged as you efficiently complete tasks but don't get everything done that you have set yourself up to do. No fun.

The following tips may help you get more accomplished in a day. However, if you really want to unclutter your life, please take care not to become "too" efficient. Think about how to use any time you free up. If not, you may find yourself even more rushed than before.

Here are the time management tips:

1. Make plans to use your time efficiently.

Plan so that you won't backtrack or go certain places more than once per week. Organized errand running is an example. Have a schedule or routine for all those weekly activities and errands for "necessities." (Yes, that nasty "h" word called "habit" can actually save you time.) Also, consider buying in bulk, by mail, or from the Internet. When you do need to go out, group errands by location. Save time and money this way.

2. Use a family calendar.

Put it in a central location, perhaps by the kitchen phone, and pencil in everyone's activities. Yep, I said "pencil" because plans do change. Record the pertinent phone number and address right along with the event. That way, if you need to call to reschedule an appointment or to remind yourself where to go, the information is right there.

3. Keep a time log for a day this fall.

What? Drag a small note pad or binder with you for just one day and jot down what you are doing every 5-10 minutes from when you wake up until you go to bed. Why? Because, just like a weight-loss diet or a monetary budget, it is easier to manage what you are doing if you can look at a complete and objective record of where you currently are.

A time log will give you a record you can review. It will help you see where you can save time and where you can't. Maybe you feel like you have no time, but you recorded that you watched television or sat at the computer last night from 8pm to 10pm...How many times did you check your e-mail?

A time log will show you where you spend your time to help you make educated choices to improve your time use. Keep a one-day time log once every few months or whenever you start feeling overwhelmed and in need of change.

4. Time yourself at the tasks you hate doing.

I am not kidding here. Try it now rather than waiting until you hear this advice a dozen times like I did. Okay. I confess. I can be a big baby about making my bed or folding the laundry. I would waste half a Saturday morning drinking too much coffee before going back to make my bed, and I would sometimes think about the laundry folding for two or three days before taking care of it. Timing myself at these tasks showed me I make my bed in two minutes and fold the family laundry in about 30 minutes.

Perspective. Timing myself at tasks I hate gave me perspective. It taught me to quit wasting time stalling and just get this "dreaded" stuff done. (Here's the thing, though. You can't just laugh as you read about the tasks that I am embarrassed about stalling, you have to time yourself at your own stalled tasks to truly gain your own perspective.)

5. Pick the right time for tasks.

You know if you are a morning person or a night person. Do your most challenging stuff in your peak time. Save mindless tasks, like folding laundry, for your mindless time. Yes, you will sometimes find me folding laundry at 10:30 at night.

6. Carefully implement multi-tasking.

Listen to educational tapes while in the car. Empty the dishwasher while you make dinner.

Fold laundry while talking on the phone or catching up with a favorite television program.

Apply multi-tasking carefully because this technique can actually contribute to a person's stress level and lack of focus.

7. Get rid of your personal time wasters.

You know what these are if you stop to think about it for a minute or if you keep a time log for a day once in a while. I have used the Internet, television, and computer games for a few of my personal time wasters.

8. Drop perfectionism and procrastination.

Perfectionism holds us back from attempts to get better organized, manage our time better, or even to try something new that we have always wanted to do. We can all learn to tweak things as we go. Decide it is more important to get started than to do it perfectly. Procrastination can also be overcome. Start first with a small change or step to get unstuck.

Plan a personal reward to motivate yourself to make progress. You are "good enough," and you can do this.

The efficiency tips above can free up time to pursue your life goals. Plunge in with some new goals and some efficient time management techniques to unclutter your life this fall.

"Secrets" to find and use extra time:

We have all heard about getting up an hour earlier or staying up an hour later to make time to get more done. It looks good on paper when we read it. But, it can be hard to keep up our motivation to do it. How can we make this work? Here are the secrets:

1. Don't plan to get up early every day or to stay up late every night. Either possibility would be too exhausting. Pick two or three times per week to do it, and you will be able to stick with it.

2. Have a specific plan for how you are going to use that "extra" time before you set the alarm clock! It is too easy to simply quit for the night or to hit the snooze bar in the morning.

   You will be less likely to quit, if you have a concrete plan and get motivated for a specific project you want to accomplish during that time.

CHAPTER 3

WHEN TIME MANAGEMENT TECHNIQUES FAIL: TOUGH CHOICES TO UNCLUTTER LIFE

There is no time. I have no energy. Fall is hectic and Christmas is just around the corner! I have gotten as efficient and organized as I can get, and it still just isn't enough. Everything isn't getting done any more. I can't keep up, and I am tired of rushing around close to panic.

Do you ever feel this way? What is the answer?

I glance at the magazines and books by the grocery checkout. They tell me to calm down by taking bubble baths and to practice deep breathing or a short meditation to reduce my stress. I am sorry, but those quickie techniques sound like trying to put a small finger bandage on that Grand Canyon called Life that seems determined to sweep me away.

Quick fixes aren't the answer. It depresses me that the information gurus on magazine covers at the grocery store checkout are satisfied with treating the symptoms rather than addressing the causes. Hop on the latest bandwagon. All your problems will be solved! Why do they do that? Because it seems easier!

We have many choices every day. We can cover up symptoms, or we can try to fix underlying causes. If I have a headache, I may need more sleep at night rather than something to mask the pain. Maybe I need to take a hard look at my life to see if I can eliminate things that are causing the headache – perhaps too many activities?

There's the rub! It is easier to crack a can of pop or take some pain medication than it is to make tough choices about how I live my life. Yet, when I make the tough choices, my gut tells me that

I am moving my life in the right direction.

For example, sometimes my "stuff to-do" list is very long and includes "stuff" like laundry, buying toilet paper, or taking care of something in the house.

I also have a "people" to-do list. Many of us don't write this list down. It sort of floats around in our heads as vague "ought to's" and "shoulds." This list includes things like calling and emailing family members and friends, scheduling get-togethers with friends, making doctor appointments for myself and other family members.

When I choose to take care of my "people" to-do list first, I *know* I am doing the right things. Working on this list, however, sometimes requires more effort than, say, folding the laundry.

When I am stressed out by something in my life, I have learned that it is worth the extra effort to fix the cause rather than to treat the symptom.

I will never get it perfect. Life just isn't that way. But, it is simpler and healthier to eliminate a cause rather than to continue to treat and mask multiple symptoms. To gain better control of life means to fix problems rather than mask them. It is harder to do, but it is worth it.

The book *Creating A Charmed Life - Sensible, Spiritual Secrets Every Busy Woman Should Know* by Victoria Moran is filled with small readable sections and practical suggestions. Her resources/bibliography section directed me to even more help. Her suggestions, like anyone's, work best if readers are willing to make the personal choices and changes needed to do them. There again is the rub.

Sometimes I am willing to crack that can of caffeine while I work on the tough stuff. After all, I need to stay awake to finish the book that tells me I need to get more sleep. I can't change everything at once. We all have to function in the "real world."

I gratefully choose to live in our cluttered consumerist society even though I sometimes complain about it. Our way of life certainly isn't perfect. I can adjust. I can tweak. I can make better choices.

Tough choices. Sometimes tough choices are all that are left when we get tired of masking too many symptoms. The very definition of the word "choice" means picking from options where each may have advantages and disadvantages.

That is why it is tough. Maybe we can learn that we really can't have it all, all at once, right this instant. If we make the tough choices, I think we can be rewarded with more time and energy for our personal priorities.

CHAPTER 4

JUNE CLEAVER'S FALL CLEANING ROUTINES: WHAT IS HER SECRET?

June Cleaver, from the television series *Leave It to Beaver*, doesn't live here any more, but many years ago I married a man whose mother sure could have given June a run for her money. In fact, back in the 1960s, my mother-in-law was nominated for Suburban Homemaker of the Year of St Paul, Minnesota. She raised three boys, and her home was described as "a model of neatness and comfort." No kidding.

For years this has been scary, motivating, and intriguing to me. I have wondered: How can I ever keep as nice a home? Gosh, I had better get my act together. And, most important, how did she do it? I finally got the courage to ask her and this is what I learned.

Laundry practices were first on my list of questions because my husband still speaks longingly of his childhood underwear drawer, always magically tidy and full. Did she do laundry all the time? Many people who attend my clutter control classes say they are constantly doing laundry. My mother-in-law said No, she said she did laundry on Mondays and Thursdays. She used bleach alternate times on her whites, so whites would stay white without getting holes in them. She put a fabric sheet in every dryer load so things wouldn't have static and stick together.

How often were the sheets and towels changed? (Do you ever wonder how often other people really do this?) My mother-in-law said towels got washed every time she did laundry and sheets got changed once a week and washed on a laundry day. How about the rest of the bedding? The beds got stripped down, and everything on the beds got washed, and the mattresses were turned in the spring and in the fall. She demonstrated how to neatly fold a fitted sheet by tucking the corners into each other, smoothing the sheet flat, and then folding it neatly. Cool.

With three boys and a dog, she must have dusted and vacuumed constantly? No. She said she dusted and vacuumed once a week unless there was a specific mess that needed to be cleaned up. Did she move the furniture every time? No, she only moved it once in a while. Did she clean the baseboards and curtains every time? No. She did a thorough room-by-room cleaning once each spring and fall. What about windows? They got cleaned every six months, including the storms and the screens.

Did she empty out closets all the time? No. She would just cull out extra stuff in closets when she was in them. She didn't empty out the closets at all. Most toys were kept in a central spot downstairs. I am guessing this helped keep the bedrooms tidier and easier to work with.

Maybe the kitchen and bathroom were getting cleaned all the time? Did she spend all her time mopping? No. These rooms got scrubbed down once a week. As a little preventative maintenance, she did quickly swish out the tub each time. The toilet, bathtub, and the rest of the bathroom got cleaned weekly.

Did she have special cleaning products that did a better job than anyone else's? No. She used a solution of one-part vinegar to three-parts water for cleaning glass mirrors and windows. She used an over-the-counter product in the kitchen, a spray product for soap scum, and a clinging product for the toilet bowls. She liked non-sudsing ammonia in water for general cleaning. After wiping down fixtures, this same water would be used to mop the bathroom and kitchen floors. It was a simple effective system, and it didn't waste cleaning water either.

What was I learning? There were no astounding discoveries here, but I began to see a pattern. My mother-in-law had very thorough organizational habits. Also, almost every time I asked a cleaning question, her answer included "unless there was something more important going on that day."

Keeping a clean house was important, but it was clear that people and activities came first. She wasn't one to waste time lingering over partially completed tasks. When I asked about laundry, she said, "If I'm getting tied down doing laundry, I might as well get it done and over with."

Her secrets to nice housekeeping didn't include fanatically frequent cleaning schedules or special mystery cleaning products. She developed regular routines, including a twice-per-year system for those nagging big projects.

I often waste time pondering and worrying about some of the big cleaning jobs instead of just doing them. I think it would be very freeing to establish a better weekly schedule and to practice a twice-per-year spring and fall deep cleaning schedule.

If I know I am going to do laundry on Thursdays, I don't have to think about it the other six days of the week. If I mark down a couple weeks twice a year on my calendar for the big projects, I can quit fretting about them the rest of the year. Maybe I can simplify my own housekeeping by following my mother-in-law's lead of sticking to a few reasonable household cleaning habits. Ultimately, we each have different lives and circumstances, so we need to find, individually, what works best. This chapter simply suggests one approach.

CHAPTER 5

SCHOOL PAPER ORGANIZATION FOR THE PARENTALLY PILED UPON

Buried. The avalanche of paperwork from the backpacks has hit. Forms, permission slips, artwork and completed homework are just the beginning. I don't know how other parents keep it all straight, especially if they have more than a couple of kids.

I have a couple of kids. Sometimes it is all I can do to "appear" to stay on top of it. Will I remember that it's school photo day in time to supply my kids with clean clothes and hair, or will I frantically discover it that same morning? Will I send the permission slip back to school on time or will I start pulling polite reminders with friendly smiley faces out of my daughter's backpack? (How do teachers keep it all straight, anyway?)

Managing kid paperwork is anything but simple. I will share a few systems that work (most of the time) for me. Once again, there is no one right way to simplify. The trick is to choose a system that fits you and your family – or you won't stick with it anyway! Here are my thoughts on school paperwork, family calendars, and artwork created by the kids.

Information

If your house is anything like mine, the kitchen is central station, and it really makes sense to keep some of the children's paperwork there. Create two folders in the kitchen for each child. One is for school and activities information and the second one is for art and awesomely completed homework. It goes without saying that it is helpful to choose different color folders for each child and to put their names on the folders. Put the folders in with the cookbooks, on a shelf, or in a kitchen drawer. Put them wherever it works best for you.

File the events you plan to attend, the "maybes" and anything else that comes home for each child. Make the information folder the one and only spot where this stuff goes! You will rarely have to hunt for school phone numbers, old newsletters, book sale information, fundraiser materials, or anything else again.

Calendar

Immediately record any upcoming school events on the family calendar. If I had written photo day down, I could have sent my daughter to school with clean hair that day! If you make it a habit to jot stuff down, important dates won't slip by. Even if you aren't sure you want to participate, pencil them on the calendar. Once or twice a year (when the information folders get too fat to fit on the shelf), I purge the out-of-date papers. It only takes a few minutes at the kitchen table.

Do you think that might work? Maybe you have a system similar to what I described. But what about all the artwork? What about the science projects? The crafts? How do you dispose of or preserve all that stuff? Here is my version of my friend Barbara's three-step system.

Art

Step 1: Display their creations! They are proud and you are proud of them. Use a corkboard, the front or side of the refrigerator, the back of their bedroom door, or any other place in your home to show off their efforts (Be careful not to scratch the surfaces of your home with whatever means you choose to attach them!) The display will boost your kids' self-esteem and yours too!

Step 2: The Kitchen folder. When the pictures sag down the side of the refrigerator or fly onto the floor every time someone opens the back door, it is time for the second step. Use the kitchen folder created for each child's art. Weed out some of the refrigerator art at this point, and file the best of it in the kitchen folders.

Put the child's name, approximate date, and age of the artist on the back of each piece to save. File them in the art folder for each child. Depending on how much art your kids generate and how many kids you have, you may have to "weed" the front of the refrigerator every one or two weeks. If you keep the art folders in the kitchen you won't want to have to run out of the kitchen to another area of your home to save this stuff.

Keep one or two of the 15 rainbows your preschooler drew last month. Toss the rest while they are asleep. Do not leave this extra art visibly languishing at the top of the kitchen waste-basket. When your child discovers it the next morning, you may be forced to apologize and possibly even retrieve it. Yes, this is the sad voice of my experience.

Step 3: Long-term Storage. Finally, after months, maybe even the entire school year, the kitchen art folders get full. If your child is a prolific artist, and you treasure their artwork, you could invest in an art student's portfolio to keep it in. In my case, I know I am ready for the third step when I can't close that kitchen drawer any more. Now I am ready to do a second purge. I am going to keep the best rainbow, and discard the three or four others I wasn't ready to give up a few months ago.

Once I have thinned down the folder, I will put it in a memorabilia box I keep for each child. This box is up high on a bedroom shelf and I don't want to have to get it down more than once or twice a year.

Other Options

Some people report success with storing children's stuff during the year in an under-the-bed storage box in each child's room. Older children can manage and make decisions about what they keep and store there. Once a year, they need to purge it and start again. It gives them experience in decision-making with their own memorabilia. If your child is a saver, limit the size of the box or the space on a shelf she may have to store her treasures. Let the saver learn to make decisions about how to manage it.

Some people have told me that they want to save *all* of their children's creations. If you insist, buy a cabinet for this and file things before they get wrecked from being tossed around in the kitchen. File regularly.

What do you do about over-sized and three-dimensional creations? Store what you want to keep safely. Get it out of the regular traffic flow in your house before it gets smashed, broken, splattered, or spilled on. I have to admit I am grateful for the Christmas ornaments I made as a child that my mom painstakingly saved for me. My kids get a kick out of them on the tree now!

As for bulky items, consider taking photos of the artist with the art. Or grab the video camera and ask the artist to give a narrated art show describing these projects before they get tossed. Preserve the memory without saving the thing itself. Might that be enough?

CHAPTER 6

LOVE YOURSELF & YOUR FAMILY: WEED OUT BEFORE WINTER

Why are we polite to the store cashier but sometimes come home and snap at our spouse or children? Why do we clean harder for company than we clean for ourselves? Our society seems to have its prioritizing backwards, if you ask me. I propose that we could clean for our partners, spouses, children, and yes, even ourselves with more enthusiasm than we clean for acquaintances or strangers (we could even strive to be more pleasant to our home companions too).

Try a new approach as you weed out fall clutter in preparation for winter: Make your living spaces and storage spaces look like company is coming, but do it for you! You deserve to enjoy life in an easy-to-clean, uncluttered, organized home. Treat yourself and your family with the respect that many of us save for strangers: Create a home space that honors and supports you and your family. Get rid of the junk.

Look at your possessions through the eyes of a stranger — as though you are company coming to your house. Pretend to be a stranger when you peek into your closets, cupboards, and drawers. When I see my "precious" stuff through an outsider's eyes, I see it for what much of it is – junk. Ouch. If a stranger would call it junk, then that is probably what it is.

Is it Beautiful?
Keep only what is still beautiful. Something that looked great two years ago may now look faded and worn. Or maybe it has simply lost its attraction as we have moved on to other more interesting things. Sadly, many tired items continue to reside in

our homes. We loved them once, but now the attraction has faded and we are off to other things. When your junk's season has passed, it is time to send it on.

Useful

Keep only what is currently useful. If you aren't using something, you are storing it. It clogs your space. Worrying and wondering about keeping it drains your energy. It steals time because you must take care of it, and it seizes you with the guilt of the alleged "I'll get back to it some day." Because things accumulate and take up a lot of space, they prevent new stuff that would be more useful from entering your life. You don't get to have the latest technology or take on a new hobby that interests you because your dwelling is already bulging at the seams. Get rid of things that were useful in the past to make room for what would be useful to you now. Be kind to yourself. Give yourself room to grow.

Sentimental

Keep only what is seriously sentimental. Seriously. The moments and the memories reside in you, not in your stuff. You are the one who had the experiences you associate with the stuff, and besides, your stuff can't talk! Take a photo. Write in your journal about the memory. Keep a photo album or scrapbook to share your special memories with others. If you still feel the need to save the sentimental item itself, maybe you could save just a piece of it. A button or a swatch of fabric is easier to save than the whole jacket. From a dated collection, choose two or three favorite pieces, and consider passing on the rest.

Is your car like a second home?

Remember the car – you are in your car every day, which is more often than you open some drawers and closets. Make this a clean haven rather than a roaming junk-mobile. Clean the inside of the car. Wipe off the dust. Clean the insides of the windows. Have a trash container in the car, and keep a trash can near where you park your car, so that every time you get out of your car, you can take your litter with you and dispose of it. You wouldn't want friends to climb in to a messy car seat, so why would you want to either?

Don't forget to think about your garage. After all, you walk through this area every time you come home or leave. Who wants to be pulled down by the old junk that manages to breed in the garage? Donate the outgrown toys. Toss the unused lumber, and recycle those cardboard boxes.

Nice for you and your family

Finally, be thorough. Be thorough for yourself and your family. Clean out all the spaces you live in. Don't forget your laundry area. Though it isn't a spot where you entertain company, you and your loved ones probably spend a lot of time there. Treat yourself by making it as pleasant as possible. Toss out odds and ends, mending that never got done, and laundry products that aren't part of your current repertoire. Install shelves or cabinets above the washer and dryer to store what you need there, and create a clean flat area to fold there if you can. If you have wall space, put a corkboard or picture frame that holds a collage of family photos and happy memories to ponder while you do laundry!

As the days get shorter and the temperature drops, I try to do a fall clutter control sweep through all areas of our home. As we prepare to burrow in for winter, I want our nest to be as uncluttered and pleasant as possible. It sounds corny, but if you think about it, even animals don't foul their own nests. Why would we?

CHAPTER 7

SNEAKY STUFF: ZAP "HIDDEN" CLUTTER THIS FALL

There is an insidious kind of clutter. This sneaky stuff hides under my radar. Is it hiding under your radar too? I am talking about old collections, projects, and hobbies — things you may know you have and stuff you don't even realize you still own.

These sneaky things accumulate together, stick together, and hang around in a household for too long. Consider hobbies or projects you intend to get back to "some day." Maybe it is a collection of tea cups, an unfinished cross-stitch project, or an old woodworking hobby. Really look at the pictures on the walls or groupings of "decorative" knick-knacks that nobody notices any more. Some of this stuff has been around for so long and become so much a part of you that you no longer even see it any more. Is it still you? Or does this stuff clog your space and vaguely disturb your peace of mind? Maybe it even holds you back. Your space and your life could have room in it for you to change and to grow.

It is hard to "see" this stuff and even harder to part with it – unless a new acquaintance comes into your home and you have to show them around. Try to walk through your rooms with the eyes of a stranger. Pretend you are a real estate agent preparing to market your space. Or take a more objective look by taking photos of your rooms and then review them. What things look tired, dated, out-of-place, or downright boring?

When you look at hobbies on hold and old collections, try to determine the last time you worked on them or really enjoyed them. Chances are it was when you first began them rather than recently. How do you feel about this stuff now? Does it excite you or make you feel a bit guilty?

My cookbook collection holds me back. I own too many cookbooks. I really enjoy looking at new cookbooks at bookstores, but I don't purchase them because I know I already have too many. If I want to change what I cook, if I want to cook with more contemporary flavors, it is time to donate books I rarely use and create some open shelf space.

How does your collection make you feel? Has your taste in art changed but you don't have any open wall space for something new? Do you find that you don't even remember who gave you some of this stuff? Where did the knick-knacks on the end table come from? Maybe it is time to sort through these things. Keep a few favorites and pass on the rest. Gasp! You can do it!

Now here is the rub. We may have become oblivious to or dissatisfied with this stuff, but we are also still attached to it! You can ease the pain of separation by finding good homes for these things. Carefully determine where this stuff would serve best.

A friend who was an eager expectant grandma was delighted to take a partially completed sewing project off my hands. It was a soft fabric baby book that she was happy to finish sewing for her future grandchild. My "babies" had grown up so fast that I hadn't had a chance to complete it, but I couldn't just toss it. I had lots of time, effort, and more recently, guilt, invested in it!

Maybe you have a friend who does the hobby that no longer interests you. You could pass on your photo album stickers or your card making stamps, or anything else. You could make his or her day! Or consider selling these things at a garage sale. Obviously, whoever buys your materials plans to finish the project or use the materials.

Collections or treasures can be hard to part with because they are still "perfectly good." Maybe you could give your family some of their "inheritance" now while you are still around to see the smiles and pleasure you can give.

Notice which items family members who do not live with you enjoy when they come to your home. Maybe you could find a niece who is starting her teacup collection and give her some of yours for the next few Christmas's and birthdays.

If no one comes to mind who would appreciate what you have, you might be able to sell it on the Internet. Investigate www.ebay.com or www.craigslist.org

Finance a new interest from the proceeds.

Be clear about why you are weeding this stuff out.

Be careful. I try not to part with hobbies or treasures just to rush out and buy more. The purpose is to create space for change and growth. Don't be afraid of open space. Filled up space is stagnant. Open space has potential. Make clutter clearing choices to create potential for yourself and your family.

CHAPTER 8

MENTAL TOOLS TO CLEAR CLUTTER

Change is in the air. The humidity is dropping so I no longer break out into a sweat when I do small tasks. But, I still "sweat it out" when making clutter control decisions. It is hard to separate trash from treasure. Like anyone, I get attached to my stuff. Some are gifts. Some are inherited items. Many are purchases. Whatever "it" is, it is difficult to toss an item we are attached to. After all, we have acquired it, paid for it, cleaned it, and stored it.

How can we let go of stuff we feel tied to?

Here are some thoughts I use in my fall clutter control. They are mental tools to separate myself from my "treasures." My "treasures" have attached themselves just like the burrs and seeds that attach themselves to my dog during our fall walks. Some stuff is like that – it manages to cling to us like a burr and hang around in our homes whether or not we really still need it or even like it.

If I haven't used something in a year or two, I probably won't really "need it some day." At any rate, I ought to trust in the Universe that I will be able to get a similar thing if I do need it later. Another mental game I play as I weed out my stuff: I pretend I am suddenly deceased. As a hovering ghost, I get to watch friends and family going through the same stuff I am looking at and remarking, "Why on earth did she save that? What did she think she was keeping this for? What are all *these* for?" and so on. If I see them shaking their heads at my ghostly explanation or if I hear muffled laughter, then I know I don't want to keep the item any longer.

What about "special" gifts from special people? I feel disloyal if I don't save a gift. Yet, it is the people who are special not the gift. When I sort out these gifts, I change roles. I pretend I am the giver not the receiver. If someone can't use a gift that I gave him or her, I hope they would decide it was the thought that counted. I would want them to know they are free to send it on to someone who might use it, rather than bury it in the back of their closet.

Next, think about the stuff we let hang around because we feel it defines us. I kept school papers and dated textbooks — as though keeping them somehow proved I really went to school. Do I have stuff from former hobbies so I can remind myself that I really am an interesting person? Do I hang onto too much outgrown kid stuff so I can definitively say I am a great mom? Ouch.

This stuff does not define me. It is time to let it go.

There is a subcategory here: Guilt by association. Sometimes I hang onto stuff that makes me feel bad. Maybe it is a hobby I haven't made time for in years. Or it is a gift given from someone where our relationship ended badly. Maybe it is clothing that is too small and doesn't fit.

Will keeping a hobby force me to make time for it again? Will an old love letter or a gift from a former friend remind me to be a better person? Can hanging onto small clothing make me lose weight? No. No. No.

Why do we sometimes use stuff to punish ourselves? Don't keep physical reminders around that have negative associations that make you feel bad or fill you with guilt. If you have items like that hanging around, please choose to pass them on and allow yourself to feel better.

Finally, there was stuff that fell into the "things I used to like" category. Some stuff stuck around because I hadn't figured out it no longer worked for me. I used a rocking chair in a baby room. Then, I put it in the living room. For a while, I liked it there...but it didn't really belong. We were past the rocking babies stage of life.

People change. I change. Sometimes I can work to be a little quicker to pass on stuff that doesn't provide what I need anymore. If it is no longer beautiful, useful, and/or sentimental, send it on!

Ultimately, I use two formulas to keep my head on straight when making clutter control choices: Stuff isn't > Person. Person > Stuff.

Congratulate marketers and advertisers for trying hard to convince us otherwise. I hope I don't define myself by what I own, and I hope I don't judge others based on what they own. Finally, my stuff can serve me, not the other way around.

CHAPTER 9

THE BATHROOM BATTLE—SOAP SCUM & MIRROR SMEARS

If bathrooms could have poor health, they would probably have about a dozen diseases all at once. Soap scum, mirror smears, dusty decorator soaps, aging tubes and bottles, and expired medicine are some of the most common illnesses that bathrooms suffer. Can we discuss tub clutter and counter-top clutter too? What about the dust bunnies and hair on the floor behind the toilet? Please, let's not go there!

But, we have to go there – to the bathroom. That is the main reason this room can be so problematic. The constant traffic a bathroom sees from everyone in the household as well as guests takes its toll on clutter control and cleanliness. Here are my thoughts on how to lighten up, organize, and create storage for this high-use room.

First, let's clear the clutter. Start with some un-decorating. Who uses those dusty decorator soaps and "company" towels any way? My opinion is bathrooms look better without these dust-collecting decorations. That includes the shedding dried silk flower arrangements and the dusty candles. If the sink area, the back of the toilet, and other horizontal surfaces are kept clutter-free, they are much easier to clean.

Next, try to reduce the quantity of medicines, personal care, and cleaning products in the bathroom. Check the expiration dates on your over-the-counter remedies. I bet something in your bathroom has expired. How many? What about those expired samples still hanging around? Some expired medicines gradually lose their effectiveness. Others can actually become harmful. For information about specific products, contact your pharmacist. Or better yet, dispose of them now!

How long have you been hanging onto that lipstick you never use because it isn't your color? Are you going to wake up one day, try it on, and suddenly decide you like it? Do you own any perfumes that you don't like? What about dried up eye shadow, mascara, or eye pencils? Perfume samples? Did you hang onto the hotel's cute miniature products? What about those pricey lotions you just didn't care for? Feel bad once as you toss them, rather than every time you have to scrounge around them in the bathroom drawer.

The same advice applies to cleaning products. So... I had a coupon and thought I would try a new cleaner, but this new product never became part of my cleaning routine or maybe I tried it once and I didn't like it. Rather than waiting until its container rotted away and it leaked on the floor of my cabinet, I could have properly disposed of it or found a friend who uses that brand.

Get rid of bathroom guilt. You could purge products you aren't using to free up space and time in the bathroom. Maybe you made some unwise purchasing decisions. Admit the mistakes, free up space, get rid of the guilt, and move on. You can have more space for the items you are using, and you may be able to find things you need faster because they won't be mixed in with stuff you aren't using. Why do we sometimes insist on storing our mistakes indefinitely?

After you lighten the bathroom load, the next step is to organize what's left. Group items into categories: medicines, personal care, hair care, and cleaning products. Find containers that are the right size for each category. I like plastic baskets or bins that don't have "holes" large enough for smaller items to sneak out.

If you have drawers or shelves in the bathroom, you could designate a drawer or shelf for each of your categories. I still like to put things in containers inside drawers or on shelves because it is easier to pull out a basket than to dig in a drawer or to peer around a dark shelf to find something. Removable containers make it easier to weed out, inventory stuff, or just see what I have.

I like using a nylon mesh bag to hold tub toys and a large shower caddy for soap and shampoo to reduce tub area clutter. It also helps if you can persuade everyone in the family, or almost everyone, to be happy with the same soap, shampoo, and conditioner... If you have teenage females in the house, I wish you good luck on that one.

When it comes to cleaning products and supplies, I learned the hard way to put them in a non-leaking basket on the floor of my bathroom cabinet. What do you really need? Maybe no more than three products: a toilet-bowl cleaner, a soap scum remover, and a glass or multi-surface cleaner. When you have all your products together in a plastic basket, it is easy to pull out the basket to grab something when it is time to clean.

Do you have a small bathroom with limited storage space? (By the way, no one has EVER come up to me at one of my seminars and said, "Hi, Barb, I have a huge, perfectly clean and organized bathroom with extra storage space!" I guess I am not alone in my bathroom clutter concerns.) Let's talk about common complaints and options that may help.

No storage under the sink? Consider skirting it off to create hidden storage below. Is stuff piled on the back of the toilet? Consider putting open shelving up on the wall behind the toilet or find a basket that can sit on the back of the toilet.

Do you have an older bathroom without a closet? Consider a freestanding cabinet, a small narrow unit between the toilet and the sink or tub, or some freestanding shelving. Some people put a high shelf above the bathroom door on the inside. Others install towel bars on any available wall space or behind the bathroom door to hang mesh bags with bathroom items in them. Some hang plastic compartmentalized shoe holders behind the bathroom door for extra storage.

Do you really have no storage space in the bathroom itself? Another option is for family members to keep their towels on hooks or towel bars behind their bedroom doors and carry their personal care products into the bathroom in individual plastic caddies that they keep in their bedrooms.

The possibilities to reduce bathroom clutter and get organized are as endless as your creativity. Let your creativity be driven by your desire to simplify the care of this high-use high-maintenance room.

After getting rid of clutter…

Tips for keeping the bathroom clean

- Keep a glass cleaner or a multi-purpose cleaner, and a roll of paper towels right in the bathroom. If you have to leave to get a product or a paper towel, you might not make it back to the bathroom!
- Vacuum your bathroom floors when you vacuum your carpet. Check first to make sure the bottom of your vacuum cleaner won't damage your flooring.
- Squeegee the tub surround after every shower or have the last person who showers in the morning take care of it. This helps prevent soap scum build-up. Choose a squeegee design that doesn't have any metal on it that could scratch walls.
- Check out the disinfecting wipes made for quick touch-up cleaning. Regularly take a quick swipe at counter and sink and toilet and floor. In less than a minute, you can change your bathroom from fuzzy to presentable with one of these.
- Train family members to wipe the sink area with their towel before leaving the bathroom.
- Reduce decorating items and general bathroom clutter to make cleaning faster!

CHAPTER 10

INNER SIMPLICITY: HAVE AN INTERNAL GARAGE SALE THIS FALL

Do you ever have a day when you feel like starting over again shortly after you have gotten up? I am talking about a bad hair day, or a day when your clothing or even your face just doesn't look right or feel right to you. Maybe you feel like you want to hop back in the shower and have a "do over" but, of course, you don't have time.

Those feelings may be more about internal rather than external stuff. It honestly would be easier to clean out a dresser drawer or a closet shelf and have a garage sale than to dig out some of my inner junk and discard it. I try to sort through the clutter for my internal garage sale by asking myself some questions. Could I fix something if I just work a little harder at it? Maybe, if I had a 36 hour day.

Instead, I try to recall the Serenity Prayer (Reinhold Niebuhr): *"God grant me the Serenity to accept the things I cannot change, the Courage to change the things I can, and the Wisdom to know the difference."* I lack Wisdom (though I try to work on it — in my "spare" time).

Would my life be simpler (better) if I could just tweak a few of the people around me a little? Sometimes I try to, but I quickly get nowhere. These are the times when I need to remind myself that the only person I am responsible for is me. I can't change other people. Instead of slamming myself into assorted brick walls, I might be better off working on me. The only person I can change is me. I can change how I choose to react to people and to situations around me, but I can't change the other person or the situation. Finally, how can I cope with my vague sense of unease or disgruntlement, which sometimes plays inside of me like bad background music?

A wise friend once told me how I need to make my outside match my inside. I need to act with integrity. Do my external behaviors, and how I spend my time, match my internal priorities and values? If I claim family time is a priority, but I bolt out the door four or five nights a week, I am not being true to myself.

Inner simplicity is a long process for me, but when I take the time to work on it, I am rewarded. Many books that address inner simplicity offer help restoring patience, priorities and perspective, as well as the forgotten art of practicing gratitude for the things I have rather than worrying about the things I don't have. "*Happiness doesn't depend on how much you have to enjoy, but how much you enjoy what you have.*" (Tom Wilson)

Here are a few books to consider, if you are interested in clearing the clutter in your inner life:

Inner Simplicity: 100 Ways to Regain Peace and Nourish Your Soul by Elaine St. James

Plain & Simple: A Woman's Journey to the Amish by Sue Bender and a classic *Gift From The Sea* by Anne Morrow Lindbergh.

Several others, including these three are described in detail at the website: www.gallagherpress.com/pierce/inner.htm.

The books I read are helpful reminders to me. I still suffer from the "better, faster, stronger syndrome" that I define as a self-inflicted feeling of inadequacy that says I'm not "good enough."

I am working on getting over it. I am helped by a quote from Michael Joseph that says: "*Remember: you have intrinsic value and goodness. You don't have to prove it by ceaseless productivity.*" This is #5 in *Play Therapy.*

A good friend and mother of four shared the above quote with me one day. She keeps it posted right above her kitchen sink.

CHAPTER 11

USE IT OR LOSE IT

I continue my fall campaign against clutter. Every year, several times per year, household clutter catches up with me. It is an unending process. That is okay. That is just the way it is. The process keeps me in shape. Each time I remove clutter, I get better at it. I learn new tactics and techniques. The process goes more smoothly. I try a different angle.

This fall, I created a new mantra and a new process to dig through closets, drawers, and cupboards: "Use it or lose it." And, "Write it down." Are you tired of hanging onto things because of good intentions or guilt? My response is, "Use it or lose it."

As I purge clutter, I challenge myself that if I continue to keep something in my life that I can't let go of because it tugs at me, I must put it to its intended purpose soon, or, once and for all, send it out the door. This year I weed out clutter with a pen and paper in hand. I am going to write down the items and the corresponding good intentions that make me keep them. Items on the list that are still hanging on the next time I weed out must go.

As you go through each room of your home, make a plan to incorporate this unused stuff into your life. Put them on "the list." Vow to finish any partially completed craft projects.

Give yourself realistic deadlines. Make plans to wear the clothing, jewelry, or "perfectly good" shoes that you have been hanging onto. Light the candle you had been saving. Listen to the CD that you don't listen to any more but still aren't sure you are ready to donate. Read the books or periodicals that whisper to you. Above all, put everything on "the list."

Keep a list of those "hangers on" as you weed out clutter. These guys are tough. They have probably survived several previous uncluttering efforts. They are hanging around taking up storage space in your home and they are personally taunting you. They are mean. They promise things that don't happen.

This time will be different. The process of listing these clingy items, reviewing the list, and trying to accomplish the list will be a consciousness-raising experience. You will look at this stuff differently. One way or another, its hold over you will be diminished. You can't help but move forward. For additional inspiration, check out a related book called *Love It Or Lose It — Living Clutter-Free Forever* by Barbara Hemphill and Maggie Bedrosian.

They offer a 5-step clutter control process: "Design your vision, eliminate excuses, commit your time, select your tools, and maintain your success." I like their process to form an ideal vision of each room on the front end. Seeing an end result in my mind's eye makes it easier to stay on task. It is also easier to know when you achieve your goal if you already envision the end result.

Another great book to try is *Clear Your Clutter with Feng Shui* by Karen Kingston. I really enjoyed her ideas about room flow. Sometimes I re-read a favorite clutter clearing book when I, once again, go through my house to battle my clutter.

Design your goal. Work toward it. Write down the items keeping you from your vision. And finally, use it or lose it. If you can't get around to enjoying or using something today, when are you going to have time tomorrow? Use it or lose it.

CHAPTER 12

CHILDREN'S CLUTTER: TRICK OR TREAT UNDER MY CHILDREN'S BEDS?

Trick or treat? I begin to fret. From Halloween to Thanksgiving to Christmas to Valentine's Day, children enter a season of giving and getting, getting, and getting. I wish to get my children's' rooms under control before the onslaught of all this generosity. My children seem to have an opposite but equally strong wish to keep everything. Do they even know what they have?

Regardless of the season, I never know what I will find when I peek under my children's beds, or in the bottom of their closets, or in their desk drawers... I find candy mixed in with hair decorations. Other hair supplies are mixed in with jewelry. Jewelry is stored in many different jewelry boxes. Empty CD cases are mingled with paper supplies. Headbands and belts are mixed in with shoes. Partially completed craft projects in assorted boxes are stashed everywhere. It goes on and on.

My children's rooms don't need to look like a picture perfect catalog page. They are kids. I want to let them be kids. They are individuals with their own personalities and preferences. I think it is just fine if those traits are visible in their rooms.

Now... I'm not a mathematician, but I don't think a finite room can hold an infinite amount of stuff. My kids don't enjoy something if they can't find it, or, worse yet, if they don't even know they have it. In addition, my kids are now old enough that they don't appreciate it if I just enter their rooms and start tossing. It is time to try something different.

My kids can be involved in the process of weeding out their rooms.

Here is an acronym for getting rid of clutter and getting

organized:

> Think like a "PRO" —
> Pile like stuff together
> Reduce the quantity
> Organize the remainder

How can I "get" my kids to think like a "PRO"? How can I make a process that is time-consuming and full of tough decisions "fun" for my kids? As we know, adults don't enjoy this task either.

I spent a couple of days thinking about the kinds of stuff in kids' rooms. I wrote a list of categories. My list included: hair supplies, jewelry, make-up, art supplies, desk supplies, books, games, toys, stuffed animals, dressing up, and craft projects. Less obvious, I included: sentimental treasures, gizmos, and storage containers. If you are a parent, some of these categories may exist within your kid clutter too. I divided "books" into: "already read" and "haven't read yet."

While I was thinking, I began hinting to my kids that we were going to play a sorting game with the stuff in their rooms. I only vaguely mentioned the possibility of donating or tossing some of their stuff. Over the course of a few days, I managed to pique their curiosity and excitement. They wanted to find out about and "play" Mom's game.

When the time was ripe, that is, we had several hours to work on it, I took several half-sheets of scrap paper and a large felt marker. I wrote each category of kid stuff on a separate piece of paper and spread the papers out on the bed and floor in each of their rooms. I also brought in wastebaskets and cardboard donation boxes "just in case."

Let the sorting begin! We emptied out all drawers, shelves, bags, and boxes one by one, and began creating sorted piles in each of the categories. For the most part, my kids stayed pretty excited and involved. When everything was emptied out and sorted, we tackled our piles.

At each category pile, we decided what to toss, what to donate, and what to keep. When we were done, we looked at our pile of storage containers and our drawers and shelf space to designate one spot to organize the remainder.

Wow! Empty space and organization began to emerge. My kids were pleased. I was pleased.

I learned a few things from the process (including that we would have been better off if we had eaten before we began). Ironically, we found we had too many storage containers. All of their partially full bags and boxes actually contributed to the clutter and space shortage in their rooms. It also helped to designate two large lidded boxes for each of them to store their "gizmos" and their "sentimental treasures." My best suggestion is to limit the space (size of container) that you let these two categories have.

The whole process was a learning experience for all of us. After all, these are life skills my kids will eventually need in their adult lives.

I also happily discovered it was fun for them, and for me, to work together to control clutter and get organized. We even learned that clutter control decisions don't have to be painful!

CHAPTER 13

HALLOWEEN CLUTTER: THIS IS HALLOWEEN, NOT CHRISTMAS!

Simplify your Halloween. Halloween can be simplified and still be fun. Though this holiday seems to get bigger and brighter every year, it also faces the very real possibility of getting squeezed out. In the stores, the Christmas decorations and merchandise come out now before the Halloween and Thanksgiving stuff. I hear people complain about this every year, yet it continues to happen earlier every year. Frankly, this practice makes me want to rebel against the commercialism of all three holidays.

To make my own small protest, and yet still participate in the spirit of these holiday traditions, I try not to decorate for Halloween until mid-October. I also defiantly decorate for Thanksgiving to give it its due in November so it won't be totally squeezed out by Christmas. And I hold off on the Christmas festive decorating until December.

Decorate for Halloween simply. A few large Halloween decorations can work well without the clutter created by many small Halloween knick-knacks. Favorites at our house include a Halloween tablecloth, a string of miniature orange twinkle lights around our dining room mirror (a window or doorway would work too), and a large outdoor pumpkin by our front door. All three add to the celebration without contributing too much to "horizontal" clutter that someone (lucky me) would have to dust around.

Simplify Halloween costumes. Create simple, fun, inexpensive costumes with some creative make-up application and dated clothing (yes, I just may have some 1970s clothing lingering in the back of a closet). Instead of buying expensive costumes of the latest cartoon characters, try showing kids what you already have on hand. Using what you already have, help them invent their own creations. Mascara or eyeliner makes anything from scars, wrinkles and whiskers to sunken ghostly cheeks. Lipstick turns to blood. Eye shadows can be ghoulish or clown-like depending on how they are applied. My kids even have fun when they each paint a Halloween face on a 69-cent miniature pumpkin from the grocery store.

Cool it with the candy. I am grateful my neighbors turn on their outside lights, graciously admire my children's costumes, and participate in a neighborhood event. It is fun to recognize the trick or treating tradition. I just don't expect my generous neighbors to keep my kids saturated in candy until it is time to eat Christmas cookies. Here is another case where it seems like it could be the thought that counts, and not the quantity.

Simplify the Halloween hype. I like to think of Halloween as a fun neighborly night for children to dress up, pretend, and have a little candy. One mom I know doesn't let her children wear their costumes until Halloween night. Instead of prolonging and de-mystifying the event, her children eagerly anticipate their one night to dress-up and pretend.

Simple Halloween crafts, food, and decorating ideas are fun to do as a family. For some simple Halloween ideas, look on the Internet for child-friendly web sites that include Halloween ideas.

Establish simple Halloween traditions that provide satisfaction year after year. We can make Halloween fun without buying the latest and greatest every year. For example, my kids get a big kick out of their dad's 35-year-old electric pumpkin light that sits in our living room once a year. No show tunes. No fiber optics. No moving parts. It is a simple family Halloween tradition, and they request it every year. These are the simple memories and traditions that I am going for. How about you?

CHAPTER 14

FRUGAL FINANCIAL CHOICES

The stock market can be uncertain. Sometimes there are layoffs. Maybe it is time to talk about an aspect of clutter clearing choices I have been largely silent about — money. Shhh. We are not supposed to talk about money. It is right up there with religion, sex, and politics on the list of things polite people "shouldn't" bring up. Right?

Okay, I am going to venture there any way. In an age of so many choices and opportunities, the financial choices we make play a huge role in how we live our lives, so it is logical that money issues tie into clutter clearing choices. I don't think there is one right way to manage money. Voluntary simplicity merely urges us to make conscious choices about our money management. If we can clear our financial clutter and stress, we can free ourselves for our priorities.

Money is a touchy subject. It is a sore spot in many families and it is often a taboo subject among friends and acquaintances. I once heard a respected pastor say "you would be able to tell an awful lot about a person by spending a little time in their checkbook." What does my checkbook say about me? Maybe it is easier to live in denial than to look at this issue, or even harder, to share it with anyone else. Money is a reflection of our life choices.

Here is my two cents worth (pun intended) of helpful ideas to practice simple frugality.

Budget. If you don't care much for the "b" word, think of it as a monetary log instead of a budget. I can't make smart financial planning decisions until I at least see where I've been. Try keeping a spending log for thirty consecutive days. Each day, write down every purchase you make. Start at any time during any month — otherwise procrastinators, like me, will stall until they remember to begin this process on the first of the month. Any 30 consecutive days will do. Your log actually is your existing budget for that month. This money tracking process worked. When I tried it, I discovered the mere process of keeping a monetary log immediately affected my purchasing decisions. Did I buy the mocha if I knew I would have to write it down later? Not always... Finally, at the end of 30 days, this log helped show where the nickels and the dollars were going. What changes did I want to make to my budget?

Plan and Prioritize. Spend a little time thinking about and writing down your financial goals. It amazes me that people, including me, will spend more time and effort to research a digital camera or vacuum cleaner purchase than they will to plan their financial future. Take 30 minutes to plan and prioritize your financial goals such as retirement, education, travel, home buying, or debt reduction. Now ask yourself the tough question: Do your spending and saving habits fit your priorities? Do I put my money where my mouth is? Ouch.

If you are anxious about the economy and find yourself ready to be more frugal, or if you simply want to make more careful financial choices, there are some great resources out there. Feel free to pick and choose. If nothing else, it can be empowering to know what is available to help if you ever have a need.

Read. For a simple living perspective on money, check out *Your Money or Your Life* by Vicki Robin and Joe Dominguez. Even if you decide not to follow their nine-step program to financial independence, I think this book will transform your perspective about money. They equate money with life energy and show the true costs of our purchases. You may also find inspiration in the sequel *Getting a Life* by Jacqueline Blix and David Heitmiller. It has a wide range of real life examples of people who have run with the ideas in the first book and transformed their lives.

The Complete Tightwad Gazette: Promoting Thrift As a Viable Alternative Lifestyle by Amy Dacyczyn a.k.a. The Frugal Zealot is loaded with practical tips to save money in many different spots where it could otherwise trickle quietly away. It is written with a sense of humor and includes real life stories about this family's quest to save money in all areas of their life. For some of the suggestions, it helps if you have storage space. Sometimes frugality includes hanging onto some things.

The 9 Steps to Financial Freedom by Suze Orman is a great financial planning book. It starts with financial basics as they relate to life basics: living, dying, providing for our families, and taking care of ourselves. She offers a practical no-nonsense approach to financial planning for real people.

Personal favorites of mine include: *Shattering the Two-Income Myth* by Andy Dappen, *Miserly Moms* by Jonni McCoy, and *Two Incomes And Still Broke?* by Linda Kelly.

There is a lot of frugality information out there. Frankly, reading bullet point lists of money-saving tip after money-saving tip can become boring. It is hard to take a bunch of dry tips and try to apply them to our real lives. Don't get discouraged. Be willing to sift through ideas to cull out what will work for you. You can make financial clutter clearing choices too.

In addition, consider taking a little time to think about "wants" versus "needs." Our culture sometimes seems determined to help us keep mixing these two up: I *need* a roof over my head. I *want* a modified two-story house with a three-car attached garage... What is personally "enough" for you? How much is "enough"? Sometimes having more than enough doesn't make us happy. Instead, it just spirals us into an endless cycle wanting more and more and more. If that is the case, we will never be content, even if we do pretty well at frugal shopping, because the shopping list itself will never end.

Try different resources on money philosophies and money saving tips until you find ones that click for you. We all know watching pennies here and there eventually add up to saving dollars. But, it is also accurate that "we don't want to trip over dollars while picking up nickels." Keep the big picture in mind. When I am thoughtful with my money and when my saving and spending habits match my values, there is no angst. Check out the resources for help to patch any budget leaks, and ask yourself if your money habits match your long-term priorities.

Finally, there was my 99-year-old grandfather who was fond of sharing two pieces of financial advice. Since he survived the Depression and beat the longevity odds, I figured it was worth sharing.

He said that when he was a little boy his mother taught him that, "Money is round. One day you have it. One day he has it. The next day, someone else has it. But, a good reputation — now that cannot be taken away from you."

My grandfather also said, "Hope for the best but prepare for the worst."

In good times and in uncertain times, that is simply good advice.

CHAPTER 15

CLEAR YOUR HOME ENTRYWAY OF FALL & WINTER CLUTTER

As fall turns to winter, grit that sticks to the bottoms of shoes and socks, damp leaves that plaster themselves to the floor, mud smears, road salt and snow track their way through our doorways. What are we to do? The entryway of a home makes the first impression on guests and family members alike, but it can be hard to keep this high-traffic spot as attractive, clean and tidy as we want it. Here are a few suggestions to control clutter, organize, and beautify this busy location.

Incoming! My entryway could quickly turn into a jumble of shopping bags, footwear, mittens, gloves, newspapers, mail, backpacks, and anything else anyone in my family decides to bring home. I fight back by using the "h" word. The "h" word again is habit. I try to instill in my family the importance of immediately putting what is brought home in its final location rather than leaving piles in the entryway. Contents of shopping bags get dispersed where they belong in the house. Grocery bags go straight to the kitchen. Coats get hung up in the closet, and backpacks go upstairs to the bedrooms.

The next problem is stuff we don't mean to bring in with us — the dirt, sand, and mud that comes in on our feet. All shoes must come off at the door. Every time. No cheating. Shoes can be kept off the floor in a boot tray to catch the dirt and water. Cleaning experts tell us that over 90 percent of the dirt we vacuum, dust, and wipe up in our homes comes in through the door, so let's stop dirt before it enters our home. Keep some slip-on shoes by the door to make it easier not to cheat, even when you just need to run back into the house to grab something you forgot or you want to step out for the mail or newspaper.

Outgoing! Just as stuff constantly flows into a home, it is also going out. Library books, mail, packages, and DVDs to be returned must be remembered. It helps to have a designated spot by the door to grab these things as you leave. A shelf or a basket is a nice spot to put them to keep them organized and off the floor.

In and Out! Transition stuff is the stuff that constantly goes in and out of the house — keys, shoes, boots, sunglasses, mittens and gloves... It helps to have homes for these items in the entryway. Keys could go on hooks or small shelves or in hanging baskets. Footwear could be stored under a bench or in a boot tray, and mittens or gloves could go in a basket or bin. I am very happy with my boot bench. It combines a boot tray with a bench with a lidded storage seat that holds mittens, gloves, scarves, and dog leashes.

Entryway décor can be attractive and functional. Baskets, hooks, and shelving can decorate and help keep things organized. Mirrors can beautify small or dark entries by reflecting more light, and they are nice for a quick appearance check as people head in or out of the home. Brass coat hooks or wooden hat trees are attractive and functional. Lighting and ceiling fans can be used to decorate and brighten an entryway. I like my fan and light for circulating air, creating visual movement, and providing light right where we need it when we are trying to tie our shoes.

Entryway maintenance is a challenge, especially in a cold climate. Replace worn door sweeps and weather strips to keep dirt and cold air out. Repaint the scuffed up doorsill and keep it clean.

I am lazy. I admit it. I would rather keep the mess outside in the first place than have to deal with it in my house. Use commercial grade outdoor mats to knock dirt off feet at each entrance before it can get into your home. Place a washable rug, like a bathroom or kitchen rug, inside of entryways. The hard flat decorative mats that say "Welcome" may be cute, but after they are saturated with dirt, they don't work. They no longer stop dirt from getting past the entryway and tracked down your hallway, stairs, or living room.

A soft-backed rug can be washed when it gets saturated with dirt and starts to smell. Confession: Sometimes I have walked into my house and thought it smelled stale, only to discover it was time to wash my entryway rugs. Ooops.

All this being said, it is still important to regularly sweep or vacuum entryways, hallways, and other high traffic spots at home. Make sure whatever method you choose is safe for your flooring surface and won't scratch it! Sweeping scratchy materials like sand or vacuuming with a sharp edge on the underside of the vacuum or leaving the beater bar running on the vacuum can harm some surfaces.

Carefully clean up entryway grime before it cuts up linoleum flooring, dulls grout between tiles, scratches wood flooring, or wears down carpet fibers. It is worth the effort. Who knows? If a sparkling entryway makes an awesome first impression, it creates the assumption in everyone's mind that the rest of the home is as clean and tidy!

CHAPTER 16

A THANKSGIVING OPINION: DON'T OVERSTUFF YOUR TURKEY OR YOUR HOME

Yum! I like turkey stuffing, especially when it is aromatic, savory, and still light and fluffy. Overstuffing a turkey can create a dense unpalatable glob of goo that just isn't appealing. Hidden household clutter can be the same way — an unpalatable glob of goo.

The overstuffed turkey may still look great, and the overstuffed home isn't always visible to the casual glance. I know. I have gotten pretty skilled at eliminating surface clutter — you know, the stuff on counters, tables, floors, and other horizontal surfaces out in the open. I have even learned to pick up after myself. I return left out items to their designated containment spots, yet there is still a problem. The real problem is the hidden clutter crammed in drawers, cupboards, cabinets, closets, under beds, on basement shelves, tucked away in boxes, out in the garage… My list goes on and on. I have hoarded, tucked away, and hung onto stuff "just in case" or "because I paid good money for it" for a long time.

Many of us are blessed with this problem of suffering from too much good fortune. Though an excess of material goods may initially feel comforting, all this hidden clutter weighs on my soul. You don't see it when you come over to my house. You don't know it is there, but I do. And it costs me. It costs me money to buy all that stuff. It costs me time and energy as I work to pay for it. It costs me time and effort to find it, move it around, maintain it, clean it, and store it. Most important, it weighs heavily on my brain — hidden piles of unmade decisions hanging around waiting for me to deal with them "some day." Clutter may be easy, but it is rarely cheap. It is easy in our society to acquire clutter in the first place, but it is not cheap to own it, rationalize it, store it, and maintain it.

Should I buy a bigger home so my house isn't so overstuffed? After all, a bigger turkey holds more stuffing. Sure! That's what I need — a larger mortgage payment to contain even bigger piles of clutter. Maybe a bigger home would even have "extra" storage space to tempt me to do more shopping for additional stuff I don't really need.

Think of household clutter like obesity. I read somewhere that over seventy percent of us could stand to lose at least some weight. I know from personal experience that it is no fun to drag extra weight around and stuff it in larger clothes. Weight doesn't feel good. It doesn't look good. It even makes me tired.

So, would more home be the answer? Or could I reduce my clutter to fit my home? Could I somehow survive on less? Would I be happy? So far, the answer is yes! I have begun the weeding out process, and I am starting to discover the rewards. Less work to pay for extra stuff, and less time and energy to take care of extra stuff gives me more time for my personal priorities. Just like wearing smaller clothes, having less stuff feels better and looks better.

Interestingly enough, owning less stuff gives me greater enjoyment from the possessions that I keep. I can find, focus on, and appreciate the "toys" we already own. I enjoy the breathing room and the peace and order from having less. It is fun to open closets, drawers, and cupboards that are as calm on the inside as they are on the outside. I like having extra energy and extra space to embark on the little projects I have been meaning to get to "some day."

I am learning that lasting contentment can only come from within, not from another trip to the mall. I am not there yet. I may never get "there," but I am enjoying the process. Clutter clearing choices are part of a journey not a destination. I find more contentment when I focus my attention on all the things I already have rather than on all the things I sometimes think I want.

Is there a better time than Thanksgiving to think about gratitude and stuffing? As my home loses it's stuffing, I get better at gratitude. I become more content with what I already have – material stuff and non-material stuff like family and friends.

Remember to be grateful, and don't get overstuffed this Thanksgiving!

CHAPTER 17

THANKSGIVING: SIMPLIFYING HOLIDAYS JUST ISN'T SIMPLE

I think of Thanksgiving as the squeeze holiday — the holiday that gets sandwiched between the Halloween sugar feast and the Christmas crunch. Although it isn't as complicated as Christmas, Thanksgiving isn't simple for the person in the family who will plan the menu, clean the house, and cook for two days for a family feast that is sometimes eaten in under 30 minutes. What if it is one person responsible for all those different tasks?!

Simplifying Thanksgiving or any other holiday isn't easy. "Simple" living or voluntary simplicity shouldn't be confused with "easy" living, especially when changing a holiday. Clutter clearing choices take time and effort to think about your personal priorities and values and to choose to act on them in all areas of life — including holiday celebrations. Changing a holiday involves enlisting cooperation from other family members. That can be tough. Some family members might dig their heels in. They just may not be ready. I can change myself but I can't change anyone else.

To simplify a holiday also means messing with another taboo item: tradition. "But we've always done it this way…" "Yeah, it would be a good idea, but…" Resistance to change is a powerful force. If you are personally ready to simplify a family holiday, sometimes there are only a few things you can do.

First, you can become the family recorder. Write down the plans, menus, decorating, preparations, and traditions currently happening. Write down the current year so you will know when you began. Next year, review it to decide what you are ready to change. Think baby steps. A few minor changes each year will add up over time.

Second, you can plant seeds with other family members this year and hope they sprout in subsequent years. Suggest simpler ways to do some things for next year and just give family members time to think about them. No family civil war. No sudden change. No pressure. Toss an idea out there and check back with people next year well before the holiday.

Third, if you have children, use the holidays as an opportunity to talk about and instill your values and opinions about these events and how they are celebrated in your family. Have you heard the story about the cook who always cut the end off of the roast before she put it in the pan? When her daughter asked why, she said she did it because that's what her mother did. When the mother and daughter asked the grandmother why she cut the end off, she said because that's the way her mom always did it. Finally, when they asked the great-grandmother, she said she cut the end off so it would fit in her roasting pan! Maybe the next generation will be a little wiser because you took the time and effort to explain your family holidays and traditions.

Thanksgiving can be simplified. It may be too late to make changes this year, but new ideas can be discussed while everyone is together to make changes for following years. Here are a few practical ideas to make Thanksgiving less work and more enjoyable — next year:

- Consider doing a Thanksgiving potluck feast where visitors each bring a dish, so that one person isn't stuck with doing all of the shopping, food preparing and cooking.
- If people won't agree to a potluck, have some food catered or store-bought, maybe even the turkey. (Store-bought food is a way that out-of-town guests from long distances could participate in a potluck too.)
- Choose side dishes that can be made well ahead of time

and refrigerated or frozen.

- Reduce the number of side dishes. There have been very nice meals served at my house where we later discovered untouched dishes left in the refrigerator or microwave. We ate the whole meal without missing them!
- Make a half turkey or a turkey breast if having too many leftovers is a problem.
- Try a restaurant for Thanksgiving! Consider getting a pumpkin pie or cooking just a turkey breast if you still want to enjoy a few traditional Thanksgiving "leftovers" later.

Turkey talk aside, I find it helps our family to make a conscious effort to practice gratitude on Thanksgiving. As my youngest told me, when she was nine: "Grateful... Thankful... Thanksgiving... Get it, Mom?"

Okay, I'm working on it.

CHAPTER 18

A NOT-SO-PERFECT HOLIDAY TABLE: SOMETIMES STUFF ISN'T CLUTTER

How can I create the perfect holiday when there are some empty places round the table? I miss my grandpa. He died about a month before his 100th birthday. I miss my parents. Due to health reasons, we are unable to be together for the holidays. I miss my brother-in-law and aunt. They each passed away unexpectedly a few years ago. Though not physically present at my Thanksgiving table, all five are there for me in spirit.

Loss, grief, health concerns, worry, and separation are part of the holiday table for many of us. Holidays aren't perfect because life isn't perfect. Life simply is. The good and bad events in life provide contrast, opportunities to learn, and times to share together.

Though material things are sometimes clutter, there are also times we can celebrate the memories of loved ones through material things. My grandfather's china dishes and my mother's silverware grace our holiday table. I am blessed that they are there to remind me of my family. I will pass the dishes and flatware on to my own daughters some day. I hope my daughters will remember the presence of these things at our holiday tables, and I hope they will use them to create new memories with their own families.

I have learned that clutter control and home organization will not create the perfect happy holiday any more than having the perfectly color-coordinated table or room would. Shopping won't do it. Planning won't do it. Cleaning won't do it.

How can the holidays be happy? Happiness isn't something a person can go out and find, but a level of happiness is something that a person can create. My grandpa created it by telling stories when he and I ate together. My parents created it with family card games, carefully planned holiday meals, and other fun times together.

It has taken me a long time to figure out that the holidays are a chance to enjoy time together and celebrate what we have instead of fretting about what we don't have. The holidays are not about the perfect gift, perfect place setting, or perfect life.

Each year I hope to contribute to the holiday celebration by striving for pleasant rather than perfect. I have been known to drive family members crazy while I try to make everything just so. It doesn't work. Being crabby and out-of-sorts and inflicting that on other family members doesn't create a perfect holiday.

I am sorry if your holidays don't turn out to be everything you hope them to be for you and your family. What each of us can do is connect with the people who matter to us and try to lose the "would haves," "could haves," and "should haves."

Enjoy the people who can make it to the table this year and take a moment of thoughtful reflection for those who can't. Each of us can sit down and enjoy the holiday table that is there, instead of fretting about the one we think we "should" have.

CHAPTER 19

LET'S TALK TURKEY: CLEAR THE CLUTTER, KEEP THE GRATITUDE

Thanksgiving is almost here. Days are gray, cold, and short. Nights are long and dark. Add the stress of the holidays that are coming up. Is it really a time to celebrate? Maybe.

Thanksgiving is an opportunity to choose to consciously practice gratitude. Since gifts aren't involved in this holiday, it is a chance to focus on relationships. As individuals, we may not be able to change the world much, but we can change ourselves. We can choose to be friendly or to be rude. We can choose to sulk or to be outgoing. We can choose to close in on ourselves or to reach out to others. Thanksgiving is a chance to do our best for the people around us.

I talk a lot on the topic of gratitude because I feel it is a topic that is vastly underrated. Gratitude is feeling and thinking about and expressing what we are thankful for.

Would someone pout if they are the one responsible for pulling off their family's Thanksgiving feast? They could if they think of all the housecleaning, food purchases, and hours of preparation that go into a Thanksgiving dinner. Is it hard work or is it a labor of love? We each have a choice here of how we perceive it and how we treat it.

Thanksgiving is sometimes hosted at my home. Yes, I am stressed. I am also grateful. I am grateful I have a home to entertain my family. I am grateful that I will be able to put a lot of food on the table. (I am also grateful for the leftovers!) I can choose to look at the preparation as an arduous task or as a celebration of gratitude. Personally, I would rather try to celebrate.

I don't have to play the role of the pouting martyr. I am not "going it alone." This time I followed my own advice: I asked for help and I am getting it. Other family members are bringing things to the feast. Don't be afraid to ask for help if that will reduce the stress. I am grateful for all the help.

On Thanksgiving, most of us will be together as a family. Not all families are so fortunate. Reach out. Invite people who can't be with their own families on Thanksgiving. Express your gratitude for their friendship by making them honorary family members.

Finally, I am simply grateful that my family will come over for Thanksgiving. Thanksgiving won't be perfect, but we will muddle through it together. My house won't be perfectly clean. My dishes and my table will not be perfectly color coordinated. That is okay.

Holidays are not about perfection. Marketers try to convince us that we must be perfect, but it isn't true. A color-coordinated table wouldn't produce the perfect family. There is no such thing out there. We are all human and prone to our idiosyncrasies and problems. I simply need to get better at appreciating the family I have. One way I can do this is by telling them and showing them how I feel on Thanksgiving.

Try to be thankful for a few things every day, not just Thanksgiving. Spend a few minutes each day deliberately thinking of things to be thankful for.

Sarah Ban Breathnach in her book *Simple Abundance* suggests we keep a daily gratitude journal and write down a few things every day that we are grateful for. I don't keep my journal regularly. I try to write in it when I remember. I try especially hard to remember to write in my journal on bad days, and review old entries so I can practice my own advice!

Best wishes for a Thanksgiving you can be thankful for.

~

Section 5

Christmas Season

~

CHAPTER 1

PANIC ATTACK: FEWER THAN 25 SHOPPING DAYS LEFT? FIGHT BACK: CLEAR CLUTTER & FOCUS

A few weeks ago I went to the mall with my family. There were Christmas displays in some of the stores, and we hadn't even had Halloween yet! The 12 days of Christmas have almost turned into 120 days — four months of the calendar year. In late September the merchandise attack had already begun. The good news was it really wasn't Christmas yet.

If you want to start simplifying your holidays, you can start thinking about it now.

Changing Christmas is a challenge. It is relatively easy to get rid of clutter and organize your closets or your drawers the way you want in the privacy of your own home. It is very hard to make changes to traditions that involve your family, friends, neighbors and co-workers.

My best suggestion to move toward a simpler holiday is this: Take notes about everything that works and doesn't work about the Christmas holiday celebrations from year to year and keep them in a folder.

First, decide what your holiday goals are and write them down. (Yes, this is goal setting revisited.) Do you want to build family traditions? Create family memories? Have close times with family and friends? Do you want to make your Christmas a more meaningful or spiritual celebration? Do you want to feel more in tune with nature? Or do you want to be more actively involved in the spirit of giving? What else?

Next, write down what hasn't worked so well in the past. What overwhelms you every year? What frustrated you about last year's get-togethers? What menus or cookie recipes didn't work out? This year you are working from memory, but next year you will have this year's notes to work from which will be helpful.

What could you do to simplify your holiday and move closer to your ideal Christmas? Focus on core relationships, activities, and traditions. Get input from your family. Ask your partner and children. See if there are things you strain to get done every year that your family may not even care about.

Consider what extras you would like to drop (one year I made too many Christmas cookies so I wrote that down). Are there social events you don't enjoy or that put too much of a strain every year on your time or your budget? On the other hand, get out the calendar and schedule events you want to be sure to include — perhaps there are certain friends or family members you really want to make an effort to be with during the holiday season.

Maybe this year you can begin to be in the driver's seat of your holiday time. Don't overbook. Even though you are trying to make a plan this year, try to stay flexible enough to change plans and be prepared to take time to enjoy the unexpected. A plan is only an intent not a straitjacket.

This year get a commitment of help from spouse and children. Start early and plan ahead. Try to choose realistic and flexible goals. If you want to cut back gift giving or turn Christmas dinner into a potluck, now is the time to approach family and friends with your thoughts. They may be relieved someone finally said something. Or, they may not be ready to make a change, but you will have planted a seed that may sprout in a following year.

Before the holiday crunch is on, check out some books that can help you simplify your holidays. Three of my favorites are:

Unplugging the Christmas Machine: How to have the Christmas you've always wanted by Jo Robinson and Jean Coppock Stoeheli,

Simplify Your Christmas by Elaine St. James, and *Simple Pleasures for the Holidays* by Susannah Seton.

A word of warning: stay away from any ideas that would add more to your holiday "to do" list. Try to make meaningful substitutions with ideas you find, rather than additions!

Try to set a budget for this year. Many Americans are still paying for Christmas in March. Are you one of them? Include gifts, events, entertaining, and food in your estimates. Try to be creative and reduce the budget a little each year. Be honest this year and record what you spend so you can track how you do from year to year.

My holiday folder includes holiday goals, family activities, gifts exchanged each year, a budget, menu plans and recipes that worked with notes on how to improve them next year, and cookie recipes I want to do every year (I have a few "don't make again" notes too!)

It would be difficult to go from a five-alarm Christmas to a quiet simple family Christmas in one year. Keeping notes allows me to make gradual changes from year to year. If something doesn't work one year and you have notes, you have a chance to fix it the next year! This year take one or two days for yourself to make plans to simplify your holidays. You can do it!

Ideas to simplify sending Christmas cards

If you enjoy sending out Christmas cards every year, please feel free to ignore the following ideas. I know some of us truly enjoy doing this each year. However, if you ever find card sending to be a hectic, difficult, or frustrating annual task, read on for some other options.

- Save time around the holidays by purchasing, completing, and addressing cards earlier, before you are "under the wire." You can hold off mailing them until well into December.

- Stand out from the crowd and avoid the time crunch by sending New Years cards or Valentine's Day cards instead.
- Save money by purchasing cards from places like Current (1-800-848-2848) or a local card and paper products outlet store. Or buy them when they go on sale right after Christmas for the following year.

  Get frugal and creative by recycling a card you received last year into a holiday postcard. Cut off the back of the card. Divide the plain side with a line and write a holiday message on one side of the line and put the address and postage on the other.
- Save trees by sending cards made from recycled paper. Also, you may be able to send old cards for recycling to a worthy cause: St. Jude's Ranch for Children. Check their website: stjudesranch.org/give/Recycled_Cards.php for their needs before sending: In the past they have recycled used card fronts to make and sell new cards.
- For long mailing lists, send cards every other year, or send cards to half of your list each year. This will keep you in the loop and still free up a little time.
- Send a farewell/last card to gracefully indicate you won't be sending cards after this year to save a few trees and simplify your family's holiday. Who knows? Maybe others will catch on too.

CHAPTER 2

SHOP 'TIL YOU DROP OR SIMPLIFY CHRISTMAS SHOPPING?

"'Tis the season to go shopping. Shop. Shop. Shop. Shop. Shop. Then, go get more!" Parking lots are jammed. Sidewalks are slippery. Stores are crowded. What is the family holiday shopper to do? Don't get me wrong. I love Christmas. I listen to the same sentimental Christmas music over and over until my spouse is ready to hide the CDs.

I thrill to the scent of cinnamon candles burning, and I melt in the glow of the holiday twinkle lights I put around the inside of my children's bedroom windows. I just dread the shopping.

I worry about what to get everybody this year. Will I find the right gifts? Will I spend too little or too much for each person? Will I remember to buy for everyone I am "supposed" to? Will the stores have what I am looking for? Will they have the right sizes? Will I get everything bought, wrapped, and mailed in time to enjoy any holiday fun with my family, or will I still be scrambling and stressing to the bitter end?

Here are some thoughts that help me tackle these concerns.

Simplify Christmas shopping by keeping wish lists throughout the year for you and for family members. I had heard that the average American household spends about $2,000 each Christmas. If we really spend that much, maybe we could spend it on things people really want and need. I try to write down gift ideas family members mention as they come up during the year. If my spouse eyes up a power tool when we are in the hardware store in the spring, I go home and write down the model before I forget. If my children enthusiastically describe a toy they saw at a friend's house in the fall, I quickly jot it down.

I am also not afraid to copy my Aunt Patty's common sense shopping-for-the-masses strategy. Here was her trick: Apply a one-size-fits-all gift to as many people on your list as possible. Come up with one neat idea, possibly one of the gifts of the year that everyone is advertising, and then get it for everyone.

Here are ideas my aunt used over the years: fruit baskets, calendars, books, and pajamas.

When I shop, I try to make it as easy as possible. Let your fingers, not your feet, do the work — on the phone or on the Internet. Call ahead to be sure a store has what you want. Order as much as you can through mail-order catalogs or the Internet. In addition to avoiding the crowds and wasting precious travel time, you can find out right away if the size you need is available, and you can shop this way any time of the day or night when it is convenient for you (and the children are asleep). My other personal preference is to shop very locally, buying from local merchants in my own community. Community support begins at home.

Rules? There are gift-giving rules?!

Do you buy into any of the unwritten gift buying "rules" out there? No? What about these: If someone buys a gift for you, do you rush out and get them a gift too? (Oh, sorry, I left yours at home today. I'll bring it tomorrow.) If you buy for someone one year does that set up the expectation that you buy for that person every year after that? Do you try to spend the same amount of money for someone that you think they will spend on you? Do you try to spend the same amount on all people who fall into the same category of your life — like all the nieces, nephews, grand-children, godchildren? Do you ever buy someone the perfect gift and then worry: Did I already get this for him or her last year? (Keep notes of what you get people each year in your Christmas folder to prevent agonizing about that.) Do you ever find the perfect gift for someone and then fret that you didn't spend enough? Did you put the perfect gift back and get something bigger (something you suspect they won't enjoy as much), or do you run out to get a supplemental "filler" gift just to spend "enough?"

Consider shifting your holiday shopping perspective if you related to any of the rule traps above. If you don't see yourself following any of these "rules," I congratulate you. If you did, maybe it is time to simplify your Christmas by bending some of these holiday shopping "rules" a little. The Christmas police won't come take you away if you do, and holiday shopping might be a little simpler and more pleasant.

Clutter-free Christmas Gift Ideas

Sometimes enough is enough, and many of us are blessed to have more than enough. This year consider simple, non-material, functional gifts that people may appreciate more than "the usual" because these gifts won't add to their closet clutter! Here are some ideas to get you started.

Teachers/Sunday school teachers/school bus drivers — Get together with several people to get one large item rather than pummeling them with knick-knacks. Or try bookstore, restaurant, or shopping gift certificates accompanied by a kind note expressing your appreciation.

Families — If you have been buying for each person in a family, consider buying one gift for the entire family. Get a family game, DVD, or magazine subscription related to a hobby or activity you know they do as a family.

Adults — Make a donation in their name to charity, or try restaurant, theater, or shopping gift certificates, or lessons, or a magazine subscription for a hobby or interest that they have.

Seniors — Try donations, restaurant or grocery gift certificates, prepaid gas or phone cards if they go south in the winter, errand running, snow shoveling, the services of a handyman, audio books, or a large-type version of a newspaper.

Teenagers/college students — Find a lesson or event pertaining to a hobby or interest they have, minutes for their cell phone, concert or sporting event tickets, or gift cards.

Children — Consider gift certificates so they get to choose, or give the gift of time doing something they enjoy with them, homemade craft/dress-up kits, or lessons (parents appreciate help with things like lessons, sports equipment, or savings bonds for education).

Everyone — Purchase disposable gifts including restaurant, grocery, gas gift cards, perfume, lotion, candles, and food. These can be used up instead of adding to anyone's clutter collection.

CHAPTER 3

GIVE THE GIFT OF TIME

It happened several years ago during the holiday season. My friend sat across the table from me in the restaurant and made a frightening request. She told me she didn't want us to exchange Christmas or birthday gifts any more. She said it was more important to get together than to trade stuff. Ouch.

We had been friends for over ten years. Over time our lives had taken different paths. It had been harder and harder to get together. My feelings were hurt by her suggestion. What I got from her message was "Since we are no longer that close, I don't think we should bother to exchange gifts any more." Isn't that what most of us would think?

Fortunately, that wasn't what she meant. I am happy to report that since we have stopped trading stuff, we have actually made more effort to get together, to catch up and to celebrate birthdays and holidays. It is more important to spend time together than to trade things. This is hard to do in a society that implies the only way to show we care is to give gifts.

I have another example. For years my in-laws had a tradition of getting approximately 30 people together for a dinner and gift exchange on Christmas Eve. Names would be drawn prior to the event. There was a ten-dollar limit. Do you know how difficult it is to find a meaningful ten-dollar gift for someone you only see once or twice per year? It also took a lot of time every Christmas Eve, going from youngest to oldest, to take turns opening all those gifts — time that could have been spent visiting. Was there a better way to enjoy our annual holiday family time?

My brother-in-law Jim tried regularly to encourage the "powers that be" in the family to discontinue the gift exchange. It took time. Actually, it took years. Finally, we "tried no gifts for just one year" several years ago. We have been gift-free ever since. It takes persistence when you try to change tradition. It is worth the effort. We now give each other the gift of time, and because we are not busy trading stuff, we have more time to connect as family on Christmas Eve.

It may be too late to make any changes to the "gift rules" this Christmas. Consider planting seeds for the future. If you are ready to decide that the gift of time is more important than the material gifts, mention the idea now. Give folks a chance to ponder it. If nothing is resolved at Christmas, you can bring up the issue again next Thanksgiving to see if people are ready.

If people aren't ready to totally cut out exchanging gifts, consider discussing the following options to scale back gradually from where your family may be now:

- If everyone currently buys for everyone, consider drawing names instead.
- Try setting an age, perhaps 18, and just get gifts for children under that age.
- Draw names for the adults but anyone who wants to can buy for the children.
- Give up the family gift exchange but pool resources to make a meaningful donation to a favorite charity.

Spend time with family and friends instead of baking that last batch of cookies or getting that final yard ornament. Slow down and be careful. Running around checking off items on the "to-do list" in the final days before Christmas is not worth an injury or an accident.

Give yourself and others the most precious gift of all — the gift of your time and attention. We all can make the time and effort to have a peaceful people-focused holiday.

CHAPTER 4

CLUTTER CURES FOR THE SEASONAL "GIMMES"

If you have children, grandchildren, nieces, or nephews, is Christmas the season of "giving" or "gimmes"? Do your children point excitedly to every toy commercial or compile long wish lists as they page through holiday toy catalogs and newspaper advertising circulars? Does your teenager yearn for an expensive article of clothing or maybe even a stereo or a computer?

How can we help Christmas mean more for our families and children than a brief, sometimes expensive, feeding frenzy of presents under the Christmas tree?

Here are a few suggestions to help get children past the "seasonal gimmes."

Have children draw family member names and be a Secret Santa for someone for a few days just before Christmas. Once or twice a day they can come up with a simple gift or service to perform for this person. It can be anonymous or not. This thought process can dramatically change their mental focus because it requires them to think about how to give rather than to receive.

Provide some craft supplies and ideas so they can make gifts. These can be simple gifts from the heart: Decorate a plain picture frame, or make a decoupage plate. Apply glue and glitter to a plain glass ball Christmas ornament. Turn a small plain wooden box into a personalized jewelry box for someone by painting it and putting his or her name on the lid. Children will be more involved in giving a present when they have a personal investment of time and effort to make it.

Consider giving older children a small holiday allowance and take them holiday shopping. They can learn to plan and budget as they shop for others. It may be appropriate for them to spend a portion of their own savings too. Shopping this way helps children begin to learn money management skills.

Include children in any service projects you undertake as a family. Buy toys with the children to donate to families in need. Adopt a person or family in the community for the holidays. Find out what your family could bring to a nearby hospital or nursing home. Give gifts of time and help like errand running or meal preparations to someone who is homebound. Include someone who may be alone for the holidays in your family's day. Make it an annual tradition with this person. If you decide to make monetary donations to a charity, children can participate proportionately.

Give children tasks to help with holiday preparations. Perhaps they can help decorate, bake, clean house, wrap gifts, make phone calls, make place cards, or set the table. They will be more committed to making Christmas festivities a success when they have been involved in the preparations.

As you shop for children in the family, consider how many gifts they may get, not just from parents, but also from grandparents, other relatives, and friends. If you are a parent, consider keeping track of what your children receive from others this year in your holiday notes folder. As you look back on your notes next year and see how much they received from others, it may help you avoid buying too much for them next year.

Following that line of thought, how many gifts "should" children get for holidays or birthdays? This topic is a little like discussing our annual salary or our religion with people. We don't talk about the quantity and expense of our gift giving behaviors with others very much. Maybe we could. I have heard of three modest approaches out there that I suspect aren't typical.

One family I know simply gets each child one gift. They regularly exchange with large families on both sides, so they feel that more than one gift from parents is just too much. They do try to figure out the one gift each child most desires that year and, if possible, find that gift for her.

Another family limits themselves to three gifts per child. Each year they try to find a practical gift (clothing, an item for the child's bedroom, or something that is a need rather than a want), a fun gift (a toy or something else the child wants), and a spiritual gift (perhaps a spiritually oriented book, video, or tape).

A third family breaks their gifts into five skill or play categories (based on Pat Gardner's "Tender Years" in the Minneapolis Star Tribune, 12/24/89). They might get each child one gift in the following categories: a project that requires fine motor skills (like a modeling kit or a bead kit), a game that requires gross motor skills (a basket ball or ice skates), a "lovey" (a stuffed animal or a doll), an item for creativity (a craft kit or art supplies), and a book for reading skills and enjoyment.

Manage children's expectations about their own gifts. Be up front with children about gift quantity or cost restrictions. One mom I know sets a dollar limit and advises their children they can request one expensive thing or several smaller items within this amount. Help children to anticipate and enjoy yet be realistic.

I know the most important gift I can give to my children will never be found under the Christmas tree. It is the gift of time — time spent talking to them, reading with them, helping them with homework, and especially playing with them with their new Christmas toys.

Finally, my best gift of time to them is time spent showing them by my actions, not just my words, that it really is more important to give than to receive. Am I there yet? No, but I am working on it! Best wishes to you and yours for a simple and joyous Christmas.

CHAPTER 5

DOES THE CHRISTMAS COOKIE CRUMBLE OR DO I FOLD?

'Tis the season to live in the kitchen... Fah La La La La... I wish I could bake!' What really is the difference between stirring and folding, anyway? Does the difference matter? Why don't my Christmas cookies turn out like the ones pictured in the magazines?

Once a year, I get reacquainted with my stand mixer (maybe this is a clue). We consider ourselves reintroduced when I manage to cover my counters, walls, and myself with powdered sugar or flour, or maybe even batter. When I am finished, I am often wearing as many of the ingredients as I sent off to my oven. Maybe that is why I have thought so much about simplifying Christmas cookie baking.

I am tired of baking late into the night or getting up early in the morning while the kids are asleep. I am frustrated when I discover I am missing a key ingredient like almonds, or a staple — like sugar, in the middle of the baking process (Thank goodness for generous neighbors!) Sometimes I get confused about which cookies need a shiny cookie sheet and which ones turn out better on a dark cookie sheet. Sometimes I mix up a batch and the batter just doesn't look right to me. What did I forget or do wrong this time? It's only a few batches of cookies, but I panic! These aren't just any cookies. They are holiday cookies. These cookies are destined for public display. They aren't anonymous blobs of calories and fat to be consumed in the privacy of my own home.

Am I alone in my angst? Perhaps you are more competent, but do you occasionally suffer from baking burnout? Here are some ideas to simplify this seasonal challenge.

Don't fly solo any more. I was thrilled the year it dawned on me that I didn't have to do it all myself. Now, it is a holiday tradition to make cookies as a family. Try to make at least some of the holiday baking into a family event with the children.

Child's play. A playgroup that my daughters and I were in got together one year to make holiday treats — kids and moms. Were we brave or foolish? The truth is the kids got bored pretty early and wandered off to play. The moms wound up finishing the baking, but we talked while we worked. All in all, it was way more fun than doing it all alone.

Just be brave. Make holiday baking into a kid event. I know I just have to lose the perfectionism. Get the kids together as a family, as a neighborhood, or as a group of friends. (Okay, maybe you will want to make a few batches of "prettier" cookies later if the perfect cookie plate is critical to your Christmas cookie self-image.)

Socialize with a baking session. If you get together with a group of friends for some socializing and collective baking efforts, each person could bring a batch or two of their favorite holiday cookie dough ready to bake. Split the spoils of your labors. After all, you are looking for variety on that holiday cookie plate, but you really don't want to be eating Christmas cookies until Valentine's Day. It really isn't that much fun to stand in front of the chest freezer grazing on Christmas cookies in February. Is it? Plus, it sure blows my annual New Year's weight loss resolution.

Take a holiday baking class. Another option is to leave this holiday task to the professionals. Over the years, I have gone alone or with friends to some of the community education holiday "make and take" cookie classes. See if this is available in your area. The teachers bring the dough and run the industrial ovens. The students gather around tables to make the cookies. The spoils are divided up at the end of the night. Sometimes the recipes are provided in case you wish to repeat any of your efforts in the privacy of your own home. The only things I bring to class are my own cookie containers. Another option, a quick fix, is to make a couple varieties and buy a couple more varieties at the bakery or the grocery store.

Keep notes.... on Christmas cookie recipes for next year. I got tired of reinventing the cookie list each year. A few years ago, I began writing down what I made: what worked, what didn't, which recipes I could double, and which ones I could cut in half and still have plenty. At some point, when I have my annual cookie list perfected (hah!), I will cut, paste, and photocopy a set for each of my kids, so that they will have a starting point for holiday traditions with their own families.

Finally, **don't panic** (I frequently remind myself to breathe). There is still time to start cookie baking early. Make Christmas cookies now and freeze them. They keep great in the freezer if you are gentle with them and pack each variety of cookie separately in a freezer bag so they don't all wind up tasting the same. Yes, I learned that the hard way.

CHAPTER 6

FOLLOW YOUR GUT: TRY A GUILT-FREE HOLIDAY THIS YEAR

It happened at a November simple living group meeting. Two women, without so much as a twinge of guilt in their voices "confessed" that they didn't bake Christmas cookies! One said she buys them or simply lets others bring them. The other woman said she makes banana bread for gifts instead because it is simpler. How dare they! I was more envious about their obvious lack of guilt than about the fact that they didn't bake.

Another woman talked about the last time it was her turn to host the extended family Christmas dinner. She decided to forego the expected traditional Swedish multi-course extravaganza in favor of a make-ahead stuffed shell pasta dish, tossed salad, and garlic bread. The audacity! I have read about this. But, I have never actually done it!

Worse yet, this woman wasn't feeling a bit guilty. She was happy about it. She talked about how everyone had enjoyed the simplicity of the food. She also said that, "After all, the big dinner was only a tradition, and her family could always go back to the tradition another year."

Her idea was simple and also brilliant. She could choose to drop, change, or simplify a tradition. Another year, she could simply choose to go back to the tradition if she wanted. I was impressed.

These women really got me thinking. When planning and organizing only take you so far, how do you simplify after that? Who would care if I didn't make so many Christmas cookies this year? Who would feel bad if the meal wasn't as elaborate as last year? Who would notice if the gifts were fewer or less extravagant this time around? I suspect the answer is me. Maybe just me. I let myself make Christmas too busy, complicated, and stressful because of my own expectations.

In Christmas' past, I have unintentionally run my family and myself physically and emotionally ragged to meet unimportant expectations that I clung to in my head. I felt like activities and events that were supposed to be fun just turned into more stuff to be gotten through and crossed off the holiday to-do list. I have been relieved when the holidays were over. Whew! Back to normal. We survived another holiday. We are off the hook for another year.

I know there have been times during past holidays where I have foolishly exchanged fun and spirit for quantity just to meet my own expectations. I ignored my gut and pressed forward.

This year I will notice and heed that nagging twist in my heart that happens when we strain ourselves to achieve my holiday goals. I will to step back and pause to re-evaluate my choices and the impact they have on my family.

First, I will make fewer cookies. That is, I will make cookies with my daughters, and when it stops being fun, we will stop. If I have spare time, I may make more by myself – *if* I feel like it.

Second, I will buy some simple gifts from the heart, and when shopping gets too crowded or boring, I will say "enough" and we will hop into the car, and drive around to look at Christmas lights. When crafting gets frustrating for my kids, I will say, "Hey, this is good enough," and we will stop and do something else. Finally, I will not whip myself or my family into a frenzy to prepare an elaborate meal or a perfectly clean house. It just isn't worth it. I don't want my kids to remember their holiday or their mother that way! If it isn't simple enough or joyous enough, I won't do it. Most importantly, I won't let myself feel guilty for those choices. I will choose to feel peaceful and grateful for having the chance to make better choices. Maybe I am getting closer to the true spirit of Christmas. But I do know that when I have opportunities to trade guilt and frustration for peace and joy this month, I will take them – for me and for my family.

CHAPTER 7

THE SHORT & SIMPLE ROUTE TO AN UNCLUTTERED CHRISTMAS

Here it is. Short and simple. If you aren't willing to make some tough choices and have some potentially awkward conversations with family and friends, a simpler holiday may not happen.

Here are some of the things that I have done. To begin with, I don't send Christmas cards. I didn't enjoy doing it and I found it to be stressful, so I quit. If you enjoy doing it, ignore me.

Next, plan ahead. I try to be done with most of the shopping before Thanksgiving.

My other goal is to be done with most of the wrapping a week or so after Thanksgiving. This gives me time to sit by the Christmas tree in the evening and reflect. I work to create this quiet time. I enjoy this quiet time.

I try to spend time with my friends for Christmas rather than buy them more stuff. We get together for lunches, brunches and dinners to visit and enjoy each other's company instead of exchanging gifts.

I also tried to reduce my Christmas budget a little each year, including the gifts for my kids. I have worked on it gradually, and over time, it has helped. At least, the budget hasn't really expanded over the years even though inflation has.

I used to bake a dozen different kinds of cookies. Now I am down to three kinds of cookies and one candy. I am thrilled not to have a chest freezer full of frozen cookies after the holidays! I now give most of them away.

The Christmas menu itself has been trimmed back and simplified over the years. I prefer two or three well-prepared dishes to ten different things to set on the table. It is easier. I delegated some of the cooking, and I have chosen things that can be made ahead and simply popped into the oven on Christmas day.

As a general rule, I use the same decorations each year. I like saving money on this stuff and I enjoy the tradition of bringing out the same decorations each year. (Okay, one year new technology caught me and I bought a small fiber optic tree.)

What makes Christmas special? Each year I ask my family what activities they enjoy most during the Christmas season. Interestingly enough, the responses don't include "opening presents under the tree." They tell me they enjoy decorating, baking cookies, and driving around looking at Christmas lights.

Finally, I think I learned the hard way that the best gift I can give my family during the month of December is a less stressed me! If I don't over book, over buy, or over exert, I am a better person to be around. Maybe you would be too if you cut back just a little. You get to decide.

Best wishes for a peaceful, joyous, and simple holiday season.

~

Conclusion

Clutter Free – Freed up to Live Life's Experiences

~

CHAPTER 1

NECESSARY ISN'T ALWAYS CLUTTER-FREE

If you aren't a "pet" person – owned by a loving family pet, you might want to skip this one. It is about our dog Mickie, a yellow Labrador retriever. As a newly married couple, we had our pets before we had our children. Mickie was our first baby. We played with her, trained her, and my husband hunted with her. At one point, we figured her comprehension vocabulary at over 70 words. Smart dog! After our children were born, there were several years where we virtually ignored her. As the children grew up, they began to enjoy her. And once again, we had time for Mickie too.

Mickie had become a retired hunting dog. She had some pain and stiffness from arthritis, but she enjoyed running in the park and playing with the kids. Later, she developed bone spurs along her spine that caused her more and more pain time went on. We increased her medication to help her be more comfortable.

Mickie loved us. She still enjoyed hopping up on the bed or the basement couch and eating treats from the table that in previous years we vowed we would never give her. Mickie tried to hide her pain from us, but finally, Mickie had cancer. Cancer works fast!

Nothing seemed to help her at the end when the cancer appeared. Mickie. Mickie had been a hunting companion, friend, and family member. She wasn't replaceable, but she was suffering. It was time to have her "put down." There will never be a good way to word that. It was a hard but necessary decision we had to make for her.

The pain of making that decision was intense, but in the end,

I believe it was a final act of kindness to her. The whole family went to the veterinarian with Mickie. My husband carried her in to the clinic. It is a day where every detail is forever ingrained on my brain.

Mickie's death left a hole in my heart that nothing will ever fill quite the same way. Because I work from home, I had been with Mickie 24-7. In some ways, I felt guilty for missing her as much as I did, a dog not a human. Mickie had been a big part of my daily life. I walked from room to room in our house and remembered her. I remembered where she sat or slept in every room. I would "hear" the sound of her wagging tail thumping on the carpet. For the first few days after she died, it was almost a physical pain. I wanted my dog back!

I tried to keep a little perspective. Losing a pet wasn't the same as fighting a war, losing a person, getting a divorce, or discovering a serious illness. It still was hard.

We were grateful to live in a very doggie neighborhood – a neighborhood where neighbors' dogs and neighbors stand around together outside, sniff each other's bottoms (the dogs) and socialize. After Mickie's death, our neighbors comforted us. I was amazed at the flowers, cards (yes, they make pet sympathy cards), and support from friends and neighbors.

I was very impressed by the kindness we received from our veterinarian at the animal hospital that horrible last day we brought Mickie in. The assisting staff cried with us as we stood there. Afterwards, they made a mold of Mickie's paw print as a keepsake for our family. It now hangs below a picture of Mickie on our fireplace mantle. We later received a supportive hand-written card from the veterinarian, and subsequently, a notice from the Humane Society that our veterinarian had made a donation to them in Mickie's memory. None of this was simple, but it was deeply appreciated.

I felt bad for my kids. At first I lamented that we had our dog before our children. Pairing an old dog with young children is a combination destined for an unhappy ending. I began to realize, however, that events like that are just part of life. My kids will remember Mickie's death. They will also remember Mickie's life. She was part of their childhood. Sad events can be complicated. Clutter-free living won't free life from sadness. It just frees us up to live it.

CHAPTER 2

THE HEART OF CLUTTER-FREE LIVING—WHAT REALLY MATTERS?

I spent one March helping my grandpa fight a life and death battle that he eventually lost. He died less than a month before his 100th birthday. He had planned a spectacular birthday party to celebrate. I miss my grandpa, and I learned a lot about clutter-free living that March.

Patience. Patience. Patience. Patience. I learned about patience. Sitting next to someone in a hospital bed hour after hour and day after day can feel a lot like doing nothing. It isn't. It was probably one of the most important jobs I will ever have. My grandpa was legally blind and deaf, confused from medications, and yet he was still in possession of all his marbles. He needed me to be there for him. Period.

Humor. My grandpa had a great sense of humor. When we would be in the car with him and get turned around in the Minneapolis area, he would say, "Well, we're lost but we're making good time!" Even in the hospital, when the doctors would ask him where he was, he would get tired of saying "hospital," so he would say "Hong Kong" first just as a joke! If a 99-year-old man in a hospital bed can still have a great sense of humor, why can't his 40-something granddaughter do a little better? Grandpa taught me that life is more fun if approached with a sense of humor.

Planning. I learned how to plan ahead to manage life at home and to take care of Grandpa's home life too. My grandpa was a careful planner. He took his time and considered all of his options. He often told me to hope for the best but prepare for the worst. He planned from his hospital bed too. A couple of days before he left intensive care, he told me to let the lease on his apartment go. He said he didn't think we would need it any more. I was the one who wasn't ready to deal with that yet.

People skills. As the nurse and doctor shifts changed every eight hours, I realized I needed to polish my people skills — for Grandpa's sake. I needed to be an effective communicator with a variety of health care professionals on my grandpa's behalf. I needed to be respectful and watchful for my grandpa's needs. My grandpa liked people. He could start a conversation going with anyone and quickly find a common ground. I admired that about him. He liked people.

What can wait? So what really matters? I quickly learned what mattered and what didn't matter that March. I learned the clutter in my house, the laundry, the paperwork, and all the stuff would be there when I returned. All of it really could wait. My grandpa couldn't wait. Informed decisions had to be made. His wishes needed to be honored. That was what mattered. My grandpa was really good at prioritizing. He knew what mattered and what not to waste his time on. He told me to choose my battles carefully. More than once, he said that it was better to win the war than to get wrapped up in the outcome of a specific battle.

Love. I spent a month learning about love. I learned that love means caring, and respect, and finally, even letting go. I learned that love means patience and persistence and sticking it out when you are beyond weary, tired, and frustrated. I loved my grandpa. I know my grandpa loved me too. Even in the last days, there were moments when he would wake up enough to pull my hand to his lips and kiss it. I kissed him many times too. I tried my best for him. I loved him and I always will.

Clutter clearing choices can help simplify life. What does that simplified life look like? The heart of simple living is about love. I learned to let the clutter control, cleaning, organizing, and overscheduled daily life, and almost everything else go. Clutter-free living is taking care of people you love and living what you believe.

CHAPTER 3

THE MINIMALIST FINDS PEACE

I finally figured out what I am. I am not an "organizing lady" or a "clutter control person." I am a minimalist. Clutter shouldn't be organized, and it doesn't need to be controlled. Clutter just needs to be tossed out! We each can make clutter clearing choices.

How much stuff do I need? I need enough. If I have too much then the extra I have is clutter. It is that simple. We live in a society where we are taught that more is better. The trouble is that more just weighs us down — physically, emotionally, mentally, and financially. Instead, if I have just enough, I am happier. Life is simpler.

When do I have too much stuff? What is the saturation point? I have too much stuff if I don't appreciate it and enjoy it. If I walk into a room, look at my stuff, and feel unhappy or depressed by it, then I have more than enough. I have too much. I have clutter. Who enjoys clutter? If I don't appreciate my stuff, who will? What is the point of paying for it, having it, hauling it around, cleaning it, storing it, and hanging onto it, if it doesn't make me happy?

I am responsible for my clutter. Clutter is anything in my life that weighs me down. Clutter is personal. It is my clutter. Being overweight is having clutter. Being too busy and overbooked is having clutter. Worrying about too many things is having clutter. And, of course, owning too much stuff is having clutter. When we try to do everything and spend too much time and energy to "have it all," we perpetuate the patterns that create clutter. We don't need to do this. We can pull back. We can even say "No." Or, can we? These patterns of behavior have become deeply ingrained in our time crunched materialistic culture. Saying no can feel like swimming upstream.

"Oh, you didn't enroll your child in dance class?"

"Mom, I want to play soccer."

"Can I have a new sweater?"

"I love my new kitchen gadget."

"We're planning to remodel our family room."

"I want to buy the shampoo I saw on television."

"Maybe we will build a bigger house."

"We'll swing through the drive-through on our way back from the store."

Wake up!

How can we pull back to find peace? It is worth the effort, but it requires being conscious. Be conscious of what really matters to you. What matters most? Is it your faith, family, career, friendships, relationships, activities, or stuff? Rank them. Next, answer this: Where are you actually spending your time? Your time is your life. Does your time management match your priorities? What can you change?

These are nasty pointed questions, aren't they? I am sorry. I can't sugarcoat it any more. The clutter has to go — the extra weight, the running around, the over-booking, and the physical stuff that piles up and spills out of closets, drawers, and rooms.

I have enough — more than enough. Peace won't be found by consulting my perpetual wish list of what I would like to buy or to do. Peace is found by spending less time doing and having, and spending more time just being — especially being grateful for what I already have.

You can to do this for you and your family. You are not alone. There are lots of resources out there to help you. You can take small steps or big steps, and frequent steps or occasional steps. You can create the life that you seek.

A WORD FROM THE AUTHOR

Thank you for taking the time to read this book. I believe in you. I believe you can make the clutter clearing choices to reduce the stuff in your life that wears you down. I believe doing this will help you free up time and energy to live your priorities. Together, we can do this!

SHARE YOUR CLUTTER CLEARING & HOME ORGANIZING IDEAS & STORIES!

Send Barbara Tako an email:
simplify@clutterclearingchoices.com

See Barbara's website: www.clutterclearingchoices.com

Or write to Barbara Tako at:

Barbara Tako
O Books
The Bothy
Deershot Lodge
Park Lane
Ropley
Hants
S024 0BE
United Kingdom

BIBLIOGRAPHY & FURTHER READING & WEBSITE RESOURCES

Bibliography & Further Reading

Anderson, Pam. *How to Cook Without a Book: Recipes and Techniques Every Cook Should Know by Heart* (Broadway, 2000).

Aslett, Don & Lagory, Craig (Illustrator). *Is There Life After Housework?* (Marsh Creek Press, 1992).

Aslett, Don. *Do I Dust Or Vacuum First?: Answers to the 100 Toughest, Most Frequently Asked Questions about Housecleaning* (Marsh Creek Press, 2005).

Aslett, Don. *The Office Clutter Cure* (Marsh Creek Press, 2008).

Bender, Sue. *Plain and Simple: A Woman's Journey to the Amish* (HarperOne, 1991).

Bittman, Mark. *The Minimalist Cooks Dinner* (Broadway, 2001).

Blix, Jacquelyn, & Heitmiller, David. *Getting a Life: Strategies for Simple Living Based on the Revolutionary Program for Financial Freedom, Your Money or Your Life* (Penguin (Non-Classics), 1999).

Bodnar, Janet. *Kiplinger's Money-Smart Kids: And Parents, Too!* (Kiplinger Books, 1993).

Bond, Jill. *Dinner's in the Freezer!* (Hibbard Publications, 2000).

Breathnach, Sarah Ban. *Simple Abundance: A Daybook of Comfort and Joy* (Grand Central Publishing, 1995).

Burros, Marian. *20-Minute Menus* (Random House Value Publishing, 1992).

Campbell, Jeff. *Speed Cleaning* (Dell, 1991).

Cilley, Marla. *Sink Reflections* (Bantam, 2002).

Crary, Elizabeth, & Casebolt, Pati, *Pick Up Your Socks, And Other Skills Growing Children Need!: A Practical Guide to Raising Responsible Children* (Parenting Pr., Inc., 1990).

Dacyczyn, Amy. *The Complete Tightwad Gazette: Promoting Thrift As a Viable Alternative Lifestyle* (Villard, 1998).

Dappen, Andy. *Shattering the Two-Income Myth: Daily Secrets for Living Well on One Income* (Brier Books, 1997).

Dorff, Pat. *File Don't Pile: A proven filing system for personal and professional use* (St. Martin's Griffin, 1986).

Easwaran, Eknath. *Take Your Time: How to Find Patience, Peace, and Meaning* (Nilgiri Press, 2006).

Eisenberg, Ronni & Kelly, Kate. *The Overwhelmed Person's Guide to Time Management* (Plume, 1997).

Ely, Leanne. *Saving Dinner: The Menus, Recipes, and Shopping Lists to Bring Your Family Back to the Table* (Ballantine Books, 2005).

Finlayson, Judith. *150 Best Slow Cooker Recipes* (Robert Rose, 2001).

Glenn, H. Stephen & Nelson, Jane Ed.D. *Raising Self-Reliant Children in a Self-Indulgent World: Seven Building Blocks for Developing Capable Young People* (Three Rivers Press, 2000).

Gold, Rozanne. *Recipes 1-2-3: Fabulous Food Using Only 3 Ingredients* (Penguin (Non-Classics), 1999).

Gray, John. *Men Are from Mars Women Are from Venus: The Classic Guide to Understanding the Opposite Sex* (Harper Paperbacks, 2004).

Hemphill, Barbara. *Taming the Paper Tiger* (Random House, 1992).

Hemphill, Barbara & Bedrosian, Maggie. *Love It or Lose It—Living ClutterFree Forever* (BCI Press, 2002).

Hickman, Danelle, & Teurlay, Valerie. *Mommy Time: 101 Great Ways to Keep Your Child Entertained While You Get Something Else Done* (St. Martins Mass Market Paper, 1994).

Intuit (Editor). *ItsDeductible Workbook for Tax Year 2005: The Blue Book for Donated Items* (Intuit, 2005).

Isaacs, Susan. *How to Organize Your Kid's Room* (Ballantine Books, 1985).

Joseph, Michael & illustrated by Alley, R.W. *Play Therapy* (One Caring Place, Abbey Press, 1990).

Johnson, Carlean. *6-Ingredients or Less* (C J Books, 2001).

Kelley, Linda. *Two Incomes and Still Broke?: It's Not How Much You*

Make, but How Much You Keep (Three Rivers Press, 1998).

Kingston, Karen. *Clear Your Clutter with Feng Shui—FREE Yourself from Physical, Mental, Emotional, and Spiritual Clutter Forever* (Broadway Books, 1999).

Lacalamita, Tom & Vance, Glenna. *Slow Cookers for Dummies* (For Dummies, 2000).

Lakein, Alan. *How to Get Control of Your Time and Your Life* (Signet, 1989).

Lara, Adair. *Slowing Down in a Speeded Up World* (Conari Press, 1994).

LeShan, Lawrence. *How to Meditate: A Guide to Self-Discovery* (Little, Brown and Company, 1999).

Lindbergh, Anne Morrow. *Gift From The Sea* (Pantheon, 1991).

Louden, Jennifer. *The Comfort Queen's Guide to Life: Create All That You Need with Just What You've Got* (Harmony, 2000).

Louden, Jennifer. *The Woman's Comfort Book: A Self-Nurturing Guide for Restoring Balance in Your Life* (HarperOne, 2005).

Louden, Jennifer. *The Woman's Retreat Book: A Guide to Restoring, Rediscovering and Reawakening Your True Self—In a Moment, An Hour, Or a Weekend* (HarperOne, 2005).

McCoy, Jonni. *Miserly Moms: Living on One Income in a Two-Income Economy* (Bethany House, 2001).

Merriam-Webster, A. *Webster's New Collegiate Dictionary* (G. & C. Merriam Co., 1981).

Mills, Beverly & Ross, Alice. *Desperation Dinners* (Workman Publishing Company, 1997).

Moran, Victoria. *Creating A Charmed Life: Sensible, Spiritual Secrets Every Busy Woman Should Know* (HarperOne, 1999).

Morgenstern, Julie. *Time Management from the Inside Out, second edition: The Foolproof System for Taking Control of Your Schedule and Your Life* (Holt Paperbacks, 2004).

Munson, Carol Heding. *The Ultimate Slow Cooker Cookbook: Flavorful One Pot Recipes for Your Crockery Pot* (Sterling, 2005).

Orman, Suze. *The 9 Steps to Financial Freedom: Practical and*

Spiritual Steps So You Can Stop Worrying (Three Rivers Press, 2006).

Pye, Donna-Marie. *America's Best Slow Cooker Recipes* (Robert Rose, 2000).

Ranck, Dawn J. & Good, Phyllis Pellman. *Fix-It and Forget-It Cookbook: Feasting with Your Slow Cooker* (Good Books, 2001).

Rechtschaffen, Stephan. *Time Shifting* (Main Street Books, 1997).

Rival. *Rival Crock-Pot Cooking* (Western Publishing Company, Inc., 1975).

Robinson, Jo & Staeheli, Jean Coppock. *Unplug the Christmas Machine: A Complete Guide to Putting Love and Joy Back into the Season* (Harper Paperbacks, 1991).

Robin, Vicki & Dominguez, Joe. *Your Money or Your Life: Transforming Your Relationship with Money and Achieving Financial Independence* (Penguin (Non-Classics), 1999).

Schofield, Deniece. *Confessions of a Happily Organized Family* (Betterway Books, 1997).

Seton, Susannah. *Simple Pleasures for the Holidays: A Treasury of Stories and Suggestions for Creating Meaningful Celebrations* (Red Wheel/Weiser, 2000).

St. James, Elaine. *Inner Simplicity: 100 Ways to Regain Peace and Nourish Your Soul* (Hyperion, 1995).

St. James, Elaine. *Simplify Your Christmas: 100 Ways to Reduce the Stress and Recapture the Joy of the Holidays* (Andrews McMeel Publishing, 1998).

St. James, Elaine. *Simplify Your Life with Kids: 100 Ways to Make Family Life Easier and More Fun* (Andrews McMeel Publishing, 1997).

Stone, Penny E. *365 Quick, Easy & Inexpensive Dinner Menus* (Champion Press (WI), 1999).

Taylor-Hough, Deborah. *Frozen Assets: How to cook for a day and eat for a month* (Champion PressLtd, 1998).

Ward, Lauri. *Trade Secrets From Use What You Have Decorating* (Putnam Adult, 2002).

Ward, Lauri. *Use What You Have Decorating* (G.P. Putnam's Sons New York, 1998).

Warren, Rick. *The Purpose Driven Life®: What On Earth Am I Here For?* (Zondervan, 2007).

Wilson, Mimi & Lagerborg, Mary-Beth. *Once-A-Month Cooking, Revised and Expanded: A Proven System for Spending Less Time in the Kitchen and Enjoying Delicious Meals Every Day* (St. Martin's Griffin, 2007).

Website Resources:

www.123sortit.com Julie Signore's organizing resources for residential and business

www.allthingsfrugal.com/resolutions.htm New Year's resolutions and frugality ideas

www.amazon.com Books, movies, merchandise seller

www.cleanreport.com Don Aslett's cleaning store and newsletter

www.clutterclearingchoices.com Barbara Tako's clutter clearing and home organizing ideas

www.CoachFederation.org/ICF/ International Coach Federation

www.containerstore.com Storage and organizing products of The Container Store®

www.craigslist.org Free classified advertising by geographic area

www.dmachoice.org A mail preference service offered by the Direct Marketing Association

www.ebay.com On-line auction and stores

www.epinions.com Reviews of products and services

www.flylady.net Marla Cilley's clutter control ideas, store, forums

www.gallagherpress.com/pierce/inner.htm Resource guide of The Pierce Simplicity Study

www.hiaspire.com/newyear New Year's resolutions monthly reminder

www.kitchen101.com Catalog for small kitchen appliances and

tools

www.napo.net National Association of Professional Organizers including "Find an organizer"

www.obviously.com/junkmail Free guide to reduce junk mail, e-mail, and phone calls

www.optoutprescreen.com to reduce credit card offers

www.organize.com Products to organize the home

www.organizedhome.com Cynthia Townley Ewer's ideas to clean, organize, and cut clutter

www.organizerswebring.com Professional Organizers Web Ring to find organizer/events/articles

www.redecorate.com Lauri Ward's decorating books, decorating training, and referral

www.shopgetorganized.com Has organizing products including specialty ones for the kitchen

www.simpleliving.net Simple Living Network newsletter, events, forums, study groups

www.thefamilycorner.com Crafts, family fun, parenting, home, holiday articles, newsletter

http://turbotax.intuit.com/personal-taxes/itsdeductible/index.jsp Helps determine what donated items are worth for tax deductions

BOOKS

O is a symbol of the world, of oneness and unity. In different cultures it also means the "eye," symbolizing knowledge and insight. We aim to publish books that are accessible, constructive and that challenge accepted opinion, both that of academia and the "moral majority."

Our books are available in all good English language bookstores worldwide. If you don't see the book on the shelves ask the bookstore to order it for you, quoting the ISBN number and title. Alternatively you can order online (all major online retail sites carry our titles) or contact the distributor in the relevant country, listed on the copyright page.

See our website **www.o-books.net** for a full list of over 500 titles, growing by 100 a year.

And tune in to myspiritradio.com for our book review radio show, hosted by June-Elleni Laine, where you can listen to the authors discussing their books.

MySpiritRadio